100 Years

The Impressions of Zhejiang, China
in Foreigners' Eyes

100 年

外国人眼中的中国浙江记忆

黄未　薛晋　主编

ZHEJIANG UNIVERSITY PRESS
浙江大学出版社
·杭州·

本书内容基于浙江省庆祝建党 100 周年
国际传播重点系列节目
《100 年·外国人眼中的中国浙江记忆》

书中讲述时间均为 2021 年

100 年 0

YEARS

外国人眼中的
中国浙江记忆

THE IMPRESSIONS OF
ZHEJIANG , CHINA
IN FOREIGNERS' EYES

序

2021 年是值得铭记的一年。

100 年前，在山河动荡、风雨飘摇的危难关头，10 多位平均年龄只有 28 岁的年轻人从四面八方聚集到一起，庄严宣告中国共产党的成立。

历史无声，岁月有痕。1921 年嘉兴南湖一艘小小的乌篷船，在时代洪流中劈波斩浪，已经成长为逐梦复兴的红色巨轮。100 年来，红色故事、奋斗故事、创业故事、改革开放故事、中华文化交流故事、伟大成就的故事数不胜数，党史、新中国史、改革开放史、社会主义发展史气势磅礴，中华民族经历了从站起来、富起来到强起来的伟大飞跃。

"红色根脉"是党在浙江百年奋斗最鲜明的底色，是最具浙江辨识度的耀眼标识。在建党百年的重要时刻，浙江广播电视集团海外中心（国际频道）以习近平新时代中国特色社会主义思想为指导，进一步加强国际传播能力建设，创制推出国际化融媒系列节目——"100 年·外国人眼中的中国浙江记忆"，通过在浙江留学、生活、创业的外国友人的视角和权威人士的解读，穿梭百年，寻找"中国共产党为什么能"的浙江答案，探讨"构建人类命运共同体"的中国做法，展现"线上线下海内外"的中国力量。

来自澳大利亚的中国女婿江添文（Tim Clancy）想了解中国共产党的诞生为什么和一条小船有关，于是到了嘉兴，近距离观看了红船；来自英国学习当代历史和国际政治专业的汤姆（Thomas Chapman）想了解《共产党宣言》

的第一个中文全译本是怎样诞生的，于是来到义乌分水塘，听到了一个"真理的味道非常甜"的有趣故事；浙江大学留学生克里象（Christian Zola）用拍视频的方式向远在异国的朋友们介绍了安吉白茶如何成为"金叶子"的历程，现场点赞中国"先富帮后富"的精神；俄罗斯诗人唐曦兰（Podareva Anastasiia）想在浙江乡村找找创作灵感，却发现了"绿水青山就是金山银山"的独特致富之道、人与自然和谐共生的生态发展之路……无论是本身就热爱中国文化，还是带着好奇心和求知欲来寻找答案，通过节目录制，这些被邀请的外国友人都进一步加深了对中国经济、政治、文化、社会、生态文明建设成果的理解，并将其通过镜头传达给了更多热爱中国、渴望了解现代中国的人。

随着节目的播出，我们还有了更多的收获。在《我在中国的电影梦》一期中，从小喜欢中国电影的刚果（布）小伙弗洛吉（Ngalouo Flogy Dostov）为了实现"中国电影梦"，2011 年就来到浙江留学，经过多年努力，获得了电影学硕士学位，现在在金华做导演。而他的下一个梦想，就是把"横店影视城"这一影视文化产业发展的"中国方案"带回祖国。这期节目播出后，我们收到了刚果（布）电影部部长克拉弗·兰布卡·埃本加（Claver Lembouka Ebenga）的"观后感"："节目太棒了！特别是我们国家的弗洛吉参与拍摄的《我在中国的电影梦》，其中的横店模式是刚果（布）可以学习借鉴的。"中国驻刚果（布）大使馆马福林大使更是将该片推荐给当地国家电视台、最大私营电视台数字电视台，以及收视率最高的沃克斯电视台，节目得到了多次播出。当地最具影响力的报纸《布拉柴维尔快讯报》、刚果通讯社等都对此进行了大篇幅的报道。中国驻刚果（布）大使馆为此还专门致信国际频道为节目在当地掀起"中国热"表示感谢。而《留在义乌》则讲述了约旦人穆德（Mohammad Falah Ibrahim Nasser）怀揣 3 万元人民币，只身来到义乌打拼的故事。奋斗 20 年，他已将出口生意做到了 13 个国家和地区，公司年产值达到 1.3 亿美元，他说："义乌是最适合做生意的地方！"《留在义乌》被推荐给了约旦哈希姆王国驻华大使胡萨姆·侯赛尼（Hussam Al Husseini），他高度评价了节目，致信国际频道表示感谢："看了节目后，更坚信这些在义乌的约旦商人促进了中国和约旦两国之间的关系。"

镜头内外，人们跨越了国别、文化背景、语言、时空的界限，通过浙江这一"重要窗口"，共同感受到一个高速发展的经济体强劲有力的脉搏，一个伫立在世界东方的文明大国源远流长的文化自信，一个致力于实现国家富强、民族复兴、人民幸福、世界大同的百年大党的执政智慧和执政底气。自 2021 年 7 月 1 日起大小屏、海内外同步播出以来，"100 年·外国人眼中的中国浙江记忆"受到了来自海内外各界的高度评价和广泛赞誉，每集网络播放量均超千万。该系列获得了第十七届中美电影电视节"最佳电视纪录片"奖、中宣部和国家广电总局优秀对外传播纪录片、中国外文局 2021 年度"对外传播十大优秀案例"、浙江省对外传播"金鸽奖"一等奖等荣誉。

衷心感谢在节目录制和播出过程中给予帮助和肯定的单位和个人，以及参与视频录制的外国嘉宾。如今，节目的同名图书即将面世，希望可以通过中英双语文字，记录下这段独特的经历，把节目中蕴含的中国经验、中国方案和中国探索介绍给更多的人。

黄　未　薛　晋

目　录

The

Story

of

the

Red

Boat

红船 故事

讲述人：江添文
Narrator：Tim Clancy

　　江添文毕业于澳大利亚悉尼科技大学，获得工程管理硕士学位。一次机缘巧合，他作为国际交流生来到浙江大学学习。在浙大留学期间，除了本专业，他还学习了临床医学。如今，他在杭州已经生活了 10 多年，在这里有了自己的家庭和事业。

　　Tim Clancy graduated from University of Technology Sydney with a master's degree in Engineering Management. By chance, he came to study in Zhejiang University as an international exchange student. During the stay, he learned clinical medicine apart from his original major. Now, he has been living in Hangzhou for more than ten years with his family as well as his career.

在浙江嘉兴的某模型船制造厂里，我和一群孩子正在手工制作红船模型。

I am making Red Boat models with a group of children at a model boat factory in Jiaxing, Zhejiang Province.

这家模型船制造厂不仅制作纯手工的红船模型，还给当地的孩子提供搭建红船模型的 DIY 兴趣班。

This is a model boat factory that makes replica handmade Red Boat models. It also provides DIY classes in model-crafting for local children.

这艘小小的红船在中国有着特殊的意义，它不仅记录了一段历史，更是全中国人民的某种精神的象征。

The Red Boat actually carries special significance in China. It not only traces an important period of China's history, but also symbolizes a spirit of the people of China.

江添文和一群孩子正在手工制作红船模型
Tim and a group of children making Red Boat models

江添文介绍"红船精神"对中国的意义

Tim introducing the significance of "Red Boat Spirit" to China

这种红船模型源于嘉兴南湖上的一艘画舫船。一个世纪之前，那艘小小的红船原本是供游客游玩所用的。很多人不会想到，100 年前中国共产党的诞生就和这艘红船有关。

The Red Boat models are crafted in accordance with the Red Boat resting on Jiaxing's South Lake. A century ago, the Red Boat was originally a sightseeing boat for tourists. Many people would not have thought that the birth of the Communist Party of China(CPC) 100 years ago was related to that very boat.

我来自澳大利亚，已经在中国生活了 10 多年，在这里工作、结婚、生子。作为外国人，我在中国生活得越久，就对 100 年前中国共产党诞生的故事越好奇。100 年前中国共产党的诞生为什么会和这艘红色的小船有关？这背后又有着什么样的故事？带着求知欲，我决定去探寻这一段历史。

I am from Australia and I have been living in China for more than 10 years, working, studying and living with my family here. As a foreigner, the longer I live in China, the more curious I am about how the CPC was born 100 years ago. Why is the birth of the CPC related to the Red Boat? What is the story behind? Driven by curiosity, I decided to find the answer.

浙江图书馆

Zhejiang Library

我探寻历史的第一站是浙江图书馆。

My first stop in search for the history is Zhejiang Library.

在浙江图书馆,我查阅了关于19世纪20年代中国共产党诞生时的资料。

At Zhejiang Library, I looked up information about the birth of the CPC in the 1920s.

那时的中国工业才刚刚起步,基础非常薄弱,农村更加贫穷落后。人民艰难度日,重要城市的街道都由外国人掌控。

At that time, China just started its industrial revolution building on a very weak foundation. The situations in impoverished rural areas were even worse. People had a hard time while important urban centers in large cities were under foreign control.

民不聊生的国情激发了全国各地的有志青年的救国热情,他们希望寻找一种科学的方式拯救这个千疮百孔的国家。

The fact that people were living in dire poverty had strongly stimulated aspiring young people across China to find a scientific approach to save the country.

在《共产党宣言》中文版全译本于上海出版后,中国第一个共产党早期组织成立了。

After the complete Chinese version of *The Communist Manifesto* had been published in Shanghai, the 1st CPC organization in its early form was founded.

1921 年 7 月,十几位平均年龄只有 28 岁的年轻人,从四面八方聚集到了上海。他们决定在中国成立一个共产党的全国性组织,并准备在上海召开中国共产党第一次全国代表大会。

In July of 1921, a group of more than 10 young people with an average age of 28 years gathered in Shanghai. They were determined to establish a national CPC organization in China and intended to hold the 1st CPC National Congress in Shanghai.

Zhejiang Library
浙江图书馆

江添文在浙江图书馆
Tim at Zhejiang Library

第二站 Second Stop

上海中国共产党第一次全国代表大会（中共一大）会址
Site of the 1st National Congress of the CPC in Shanghai

江添文在上海中共一大会址

Tim at the Site of the 1st National Congress of the CPC in Shanghai

　　1921 年 7 月，位于上海兴业路 76 号的这座小楼里来了 13 位年轻人，还有 2 位外国人，他们因为一场会议聚集在这里。与会者有着不同的家庭背景、教育背景。他们有的是海归，有的是前清官员或富裕农民家的后代。没有人知道未来会怎么样，但他们知道眼下干的这件事很伟大，很迫切，但也很危险。这 13 位年轻人中，就有后来的中国共产党领导人毛泽东，年仅 28 岁的他是党代表之一，也是会议记录员。就在会议召开期间，危险发生了。

江添文在上海中共一大会址
Tim at the Site of the 1st National Congress of the CPC in Shanghai

In a small building at No. 76 Xingye Road, Shanghai, in July, 1921, 13 young individuals along with two foreigners gathered here for a meeting. The attendees had different social and educational backgrounds. Some were overseas returnees, some were the descendants of officials of the Qing Dynasty or rich farmers. They had no idea what would happen in the future, but they knew that their cause was great, urgent and dangerous. Among these 13 young individuals, there was a 28-year-old delegate and meeting recorder Mao Zedong, who later became the leader of the CPC. During the meeting, the danger did emerge.

江添文在上海中共一大会址
Tim at the Site of the 1st National Congress of the CPC in Shanghai

全国重点文物保护单位

中国共产党第一次
全国代表大会会址

中华人民共和国国务院
一九六一年三月四日公布

106
號六另百一

南湖红船

The Red Boat on the South Lake

　　在嘉兴南湖边，我遇到了另一位一大代表王尽美的长孙王明华教授。王教授讲道：

　　By the South Lake, I met Professor Wang Minghua, the eldest grandson of Wang Jinmei who was also one of the delegates. Professor Wang said,

　　　建议会议继续到南湖举行的，是一位年轻的女士，当时她就坐在船头来保障他们的安全。她建议准备一副麻将牌，万一有什么情况，她就敲敲门，门一敲，里面就假装在玩麻将，而且声音越大越好。会议进行得很顺利。

　　　A young lady proposed to continue the meeting at South Lake. She sat at the bow of the boat to keep watch while the delegates held their meeting inside. She suggested the delegates prepare a set of mahjong. She would knock on the door for any emergency situation, which was a signal for delegates to pretend to play mahjong and to make noise. The meeting proceeded peacefully.

王明华教授向江添文讲述那段历史

Professor Wang Minghua talking with Tim about the history at that time

就这样，中国共产党第一次全国代表大会从上海转移到浙江嘉兴继续召开并胜利结束。会议选举出了中央局领导班子。当天，红船上的会议一直开到傍晚，最后，与会代表喊出了"人类的解放者万岁"等口号，直到会议结束。

The 1st National Congress of the Communist Party of China was concluded successfully with its venue shifted from Shanghai to Jiaxing, Zhejiang. The meeting elected members of the CPC Central Bureau. The meeting was held on the Red Boat till dusk. The delegates chanted slogans such as "Long live the liberators of mankind" until the end of the meeting.

南湖红船

Red Boat on the South Lake

南湖革命纪念馆

Memorial Hall of Revolution at South Lake

江添文参观红船
Tim visiting the Red Boat

然而，革命不是请客吃饭，这件事是极其艰难的，甚至会有流血牺牲。我来到南湖革命纪念馆，领略革命的壮举。

Revolution, nothing like a dinner invitation, is extremely tough and even involves bloodshed and sacrifices. I came to the Memorial Hall of Revolution at South Lake to learn about those great moves of the revolution.

经过100年，"红船精神"的种子早已经在中国扎根，并在中国结出果实，哺育着中国人民。正如毛泽东同志所说："星星之火，可以燎原。"如今中国共产党已经是世界上第一大政党。

After a century, the Red Boat Spirit has already taken root firmly in China and grown fruitful results which greatly enrich Chinese people. Just as Mao Zedong said: "A single spark can start a prairie fire." The CPC is now the largest political party in the world.

江添文在南湖革命纪念馆前

Tim in front of the Memorial Hall of Revolution at South Lake

1949 年，也就是那场重要会议 28 年后，中华人民共和国成立了。当时的中国共产党最高领导人毛泽东曾在给另外一位参加中共一大的代表写的密信中这样写道："吾兄系本公司发起人之一，现公司生意兴隆，望速前来参与经营。"

The People's Republic of China was founded in 1949, 28 years after the Red Boat meeting. Mao Zedong, the CPC top leader at that time, wrote in a secret letter to another delegate who attended the 1st National Congress of the CPC, "My brother, you are one of the founders of our company. Our business is booming now. I hope you can join us soon."

收到信的这位代表，就是当初提议到浙江嘉兴继续开会的那名女子王会悟的丈夫——李达。他一收到信，就知道毛泽东说的暗语中的"公司"指的是"中国共产党"。

The receiver of this letter was Li Da——the husband of Wang Huiwu who proposed to continue the meeting in Jiaxing, Zhejiang. Once he read the letter, he realized that Mao Zedong implied the CPC when referring to the company.

瞬间百年，如果中国共产党是一家公司，它从最开始的 50 多个员工，发展到现在的 9500 多万员工，这真的是一个创举，经历住了时间的考验。

In the past one hundred years, if the CPC were to be regarded as a company, it would have developed from the initial 50 or so employees to over 95 million employees for now. It is a great achievement which has fully withstood the test of time.

The

Taste

of

Truth

真理的味道

讲述人：汤姆

Narrator：Thomas Chapman (Tom)

　　汤姆，来自英国，目前是浙江工业大学的一名教师。他研究生就读于英国约克大学，专业是当代历史与国际政治，对《共产党宣言》的研究是他研究生课程里的一部分。

　　Tom comes from the United Kingdom. Currently, he is a lecturer at Zhejiang University of Technology. Majoring in Contemporary History and International Politics, he completed his postgraduate studies at the University of York. And the study of *The Communist Manifesto* was included in his postgraduate courses.

汤姆在义乌国际商贸城
Tom in Yiwu International Trade City

　　义乌在中国东部的浙江省，是世界小商品之都、经济繁荣之城，是梦想之地。来自世界各地的商人都会选择到义乌做生意。

　　Yiwu, located in East China's Zhejiang Province, is the world's capital of small commodities, a city of economic prosperity, as well as a land of dreams. Businessmen from all over the world will choose to do business in Yiwu.

　　但我作为一个外国人来义乌，讲的是另外一个伟大的故事，是你不知道的故事。

　　However, as a foreigner, I came to Yiwu to tell you another great story you've never heard about before.

汤姆被陈望道的故事所吸引

Tom being attracted by Chen Wangdao's story

　　时间回到 1848 年，《共产党宣言》在英国正式出版。70 多年以后，一个浙江义乌人将《共产党宣言》翻译成中文。

Dating back to 1848, *The Communist Manifesto* was officially published in the UK. Over 70 years later, a native from Yiwu translated *The Communist Manifesto* into Chinese.

　　这个义乌人就是陈望道。我意外地发现义乌竟然是《共产党宣言》中文全译本的翻译地。义乌的这段历史是不是刷新了你对义乌的认识？它背后的故事也相当吸引人。

This man from Yiwu named Chen Wangdao is the translator of the first complete Chinese version of *The Communist Manifesto*. I found Yiwu is the place where it was translated. Has this fact refreshed your idea on Yiwu? The story behind is also quite fascinating.

汤姆前往分水塘村探寻历史足迹

Tom going to Fenshuitang Village to explore the historical footprints

我来自英国，已经在中国工作了 3 年，去年（2020 年）来到杭州，读研究生期间学习的是当代历史和国际政治，其间学过卡尔·马克思和弗里德里希·恩格斯的《共产党宣言》。在听说义乌人陈望道是第一个中文版的《共产党宣言》（全译本）的翻译者后，我很想去了解这个人和他的故事。于是，我驱车前往义乌分水塘村。

I come from the UK and have been working in China for three years. I moved to Hangzhou last year. I studied Contemporary History and International Politics as a graduate student, and learned about *The Communist Manifesto* by Carl Marx and Friedrich Engels. After knowing that Yiwunese Chen Wangdao, who is the translator of the first complete Chinese version of *The Communist Manifesto*, I want to know more about this man and his story. Therefore, I hit the road to Fenshuitang Village, in Yiwu.

100 多年前（1891 年），义乌人陈望道就出生在这个村落里。今天，我将去拜访陈望道的一位亲属，听其讲述更多陈望道的故事。

Over one hundred years ago (1891), Chen Wangdao was born in this village. Today, I will visit a relative of Chen Wangdao and get to know more about Chen's stories.

汤姆拜访陈望道的亲戚

Tom visiting a relative of Chen Wangdao

陈望道的亲属、义乌党史办工作人员陈祥有陪同我走进陈望道故居，他向我讲道：

Chen Xiangyou, a relative of Chen Wangdao, accompanied me to walk into Chen Wangdao's former residence and said,

这个房子是 1909 年造好的，中间这个三间是陈望道的。陈望道的家庭在我们当地算是一等一的家庭，经济条件也好，为人处世也好，各个方面都算比较好的。（当时）陈望道准备出国，他先去了上海，然后到了杭州的之江大学（现浙江大学之江校区）补习英语。1915 年 2 月他到日本留学，在日本留学期间，他非常认真，也非常努力，他获得了日本中央大学法学学士学位以后就回到了国内。

This house was built in 1909, while the three rooms in the middle were used by Chen Wangdao. Chen Wangdao was from a highly-regarded family in the local area with good financial condition and reputation. Chen Wangdao was then preparing for studying abroad. He went to Shanghai first and then went to Hangchow Christian College (now Zhijiang Campus of Zhejiang University) in Hangzhou for learning English. In February 1915, he went to study in Japan. He studied hard during that period. After obtaining a law degree from Chuo University in Japan, he returned to China.

20 世纪早期，中国近代工业才刚刚起步，基础非常薄弱。农村更加贫穷落后。人民艰难度日，重要城市的街道都由外国人掌控。国家的羸弱，强烈地刺激了全国各地的有志青年，他们希望寻找一种科学的方式，拯救这个国家。

Early in the 20th century, China just started its industrial revolution building on a shaky foundation. The situations in impoverished rural areas were even worse. People had a hard time while strategic areas in large cities were under foreign control. The fact that people were living in dire poverty had strongly stimulated aspiring young people across China, striving to find a scientific approach to save the country.

陈望道的亲戚陈祥有和汤姆在陈望道故居
Chen Xiangyou, Chen Wangdao's relative, and Tom in Chen Wangdao's former residence

此时，《共产党宣言》的英文版和日文版已经传到了中国，那找谁来翻译中文版的《共产党宣言》（全译本）好呢？带着这样的疑问，我给陈望道之子陈振新教授打了个电话。

At that time, the English and Japanese versions of *The Communist Manifesto* had already been introduced to China. Well, who should be the one to translate *The Communist Manifesto* into Chinese? With such questions in mind, I called Professor Chen Zhenxin, the son of Chen Wangdao.

汤姆与陈望道之子陈振新教授视频连线

Video connection between Tom and Professor Chen Zhenxin, son of Chen Wangdao

陈振新教授说：

Professor Chen Zhenxin said,

当时邵力子为什么会推荐我父亲来翻译这个《共产党宣言》呢？要翻译这本小册子，第一个条件就是要对马克思主义有比较深的了解；第二个条件是要精通德文、日文、英文这三门外语中的一门；第三个条件是对汉语文学素养（要求）比较高。

Why did Shao Lizi recommend my father to translate *The Communist Manifesto* into Chinese? To translate this book well, the translator is firstly required to have a deep understanding of Marxism. Second, the translator should be proficient in one of the following three languages: German, Japanese or English. Third, the translator should be a master in Chinese as well.

收到翻译的邀约让陈望道既感意外，又觉兴奋，他拿着《共产党宣言》的英文版和日文版回到老家，一头扎进分水塘的老宅，开始《共产党宣言》的翻译。

Chen Wangdao was surprised and excited by being invited for the translation. He took the English and Japanese versions of *The Communist Manifesto* to his hometown, and began to translate *The Communist Manifesto* in his old shed in Fenshuitang Village of Yiwu.

在陈望道翻译期间，发生了一件趣事。

Something interesting happened when Chen Wangdao was translating.

陈振新教授对我讲道：

Professor Chen Zhenxin told me,

因为（陈望道）是白天黑夜连轴转，所以没有几天，人就瘦了一圈。我祖母用糯米包了几个粽子，再加上一点我们家乡盛产的红糖，想给他补补身体。过了一会，她想我父亲应该吃得差不多了，就去收拾碗碟。一看，"你这个嘴巴上都是黑乎乎的？怎么回事啊？"我父亲自己也不知道，实在是因为他思想过于集中，就把这个粽子蘸着墨汁吃下去，自己还一点感觉都没有，还说好甜好甜。

Chen Wangdao worked around the clock, so he lost considerable weight within a few days. Then my grandmother made some zongzi, sided with local brown sugar for providing nutrition. After a while, she thought my father must have finished, so she went to clean up the dishes. She was surprised and said, "your mouth turned black, what happened?" Even my father had no idea. He was so absorbed in his work that he dipped the zongzi into the ink and ate it. He didn't notice anything wrong and kept saying "the zongzi is so sweet!"

这就是"真理的味道非常甜"的来源。

That's where the saying comes from: The taste of truth is sweet.

陈祥有向汤姆介绍陈望道老家的柴房

Chen Xiangyou introducing to Tom the old shed in Chen Wangdao's home

随后，陈祥有带着我来到了柴房，讲道：

这就是我们讲的柴房，就是陈望道先生100年前翻译《共产党宣言》的地方。当时的条件是很艰苦的，一张小木桌白天当办公桌，晚上这些东西拿走，褥子一铺，他就当床了。想到一个词，或者一句话，他马上就站起来把它写下来。他于1920年2月回家，经过两个多月时间，到1920年4月下旬，他基本完成了翻译。然后他带着译稿到上海。1920年8月，中文版《共产党宣言》（全译本）第一版出版。

汤姆参观陈望道老家
Tom visiting Chen Wangdao's home

Then Chen Xiangyou took me to the woodshed and said,

This is the old shed where Chen Wangdao translated *The Communist Manifesto* one hundred years ago. It was pretty tough back then. He worked on a small wooden table during the daytime and cleared it up at night. He slept on top of it with a quilt. Whenever a word or a sentence crossed his mind, he would stand up and write it down immediately. He returned home in February 1920, after more than two months, he had completed the translation in late April of the same year. Then he took the translation script to Shanghai. In August 1920, the first Chinese version of *The Communist Manifesto* was published.

汤姆手拿《共产党宣言》

Tom holding *The Communist Manifesto*

陈望道翻译的《共产党宣言》出版一年后，中国共产党成立。

One year after Chen Wangdao's translation of *The Communist Manifesto* was published, the Communist Party of China was founded.

1936 年 10 月，毛泽东与美国记者埃德加·斯诺说："有三本书特别深刻地铭记在我的心中，使我树立起对马克思主义的信仰，其中一本就是《共产党宣言》。"

In October 1936, Mao Zedong told the American journalist Edgar Snow, "There are three books that are deeply engraved on my mind forming my belief in Marxism. One of them is the complete Chinese version of *The Communist Manifesto*."

作为一个外国人，我不禁感叹于浙江发生的这个看似平凡但意义重大的故事。了解这个故事之后，我对中国有了更深的了解。

As a foreigner, I can't help marveling at the seemingly ordinary but significant story in Zhejiang. After I learned about this story, I have obtained a deeper understanding of China.

Mum's

China

Ties

我母亲的
中国情缘

我希望我配得上这样一块奖牌，这是一份无上的荣誉。

Well, I wish I deserve such a medal. It's such a great honor.

是的，它真的……沉甸甸的。

Yes, it's really... very heavy.

伊莎白·柯鲁克——我的母亲回应道。

My mother, Isabel replied.

2021 年 7 月 1 日，以高帆命名的摄影艺术馆暨纪念馆在浙江开馆了。艺术馆收藏的《中国摄影史》中，有 48 卷是我父母大卫·柯鲁克与伊莎白·柯鲁克夫妇的卷宗。

The Photography Museum named after Gao Fan opened in Zhejiang on July 1, 2021. One of its holdings is entitled *The History of Chinese Photography*, 48 volumes of which are archives of my parents David and Isabel Crook.

1947 年 11 月，我的母亲伊莎白回到中国，来到解放区的十里店。

In November 1947, my mother came to China and arrived at Shilidian (Ten Mile Inn) village in a liberated area.

这一年，广袤的中国解放区农村正在掀起一场如火如荼的改革。

This year, a turbulent reform was taking place in China's extensive rural liberated areas.

年轻时的伊莎白
Isabel in her youth

当时我母亲正在伦敦政治经济学院攻读人类学博士学位。当她听到来自中国的消息后，毅然放弃了安逸的生活，登上了驶向中国的轮船。

My mother was working on a PhD in anthropology at the London School of Economics back then. When she heard of the news from China, she abandoned her comfortable life in London and embarked on a ship bound for China.

那时，我母亲不会想到，要在此次远航的目的地——中国度过她的余生。

My mother could never have guessed she would spend the rest of her life in China.

伊莎白在十里店

Isabel in Shilidian Village

> 我想回到中国继续从事人类学研究，我们感觉这个改革是在改变社会，而不仅仅是打败敌人，所以我们认为研究这个很重要。
>
> I wanted to return to China to continue my anthropological studies. We thought that this land reform was begining changing a society, not just overthrown the enemy. So we thought it's very important to study and write about it.

我母亲激动地说道。

Said my mother excitedly.

1947 年 11 月，我父母进入晋冀鲁豫解放区十里店。十里店是太行山脚下一个偏远的小山村，位于河北武安市。

In November 1947, my parents came to Shilidian Village in a liberated area of Shanxi, Hebei, Shandong and Henan Provinces. Shilidian Village was a remote village sitting at the foot of the Taihang Mountains of Wu'an City in Hebei Province.

柯鲁克夫妇旧居

David and Isabel Crook's old residence

柯马凯和他的母亲伊莎白一起翻看相册

Michael Crook and his mother Isabel, looking through the album

我的母亲对当时的十里店有一段描述，她说：

My mother once talked about Shilidian Village,

我们乘坐的骡车颠簸地穿过十分雅致的南门，在这扇雅致的拱门上方写了一行歌词："毛泽东是中国人民的大救星。"

We arrived by mule cart passing through the exquisite south gate of the village. In bold white letters above the graceful arch was a line from a popular folk song "Mao Zedong is the great savior of the Chinese people."

柯鲁克夫妇的历史文献让国际社会了解到中国的真实情况

The historical documents of the Crooks, telling the world the truth about the real situation in China

　　我来到十里店我父母住过的地方。当时在这里，我的父母与农民吃住在一起，白天挨家挨户采访、拍照，晚上在煤油灯下用笔、打字机做记录。他们在这里整整住了八个月，拍下了 700 多张照片，完成了历史文献《十里店——中国一个村庄的革命》《十里店——中国一个村庄的群众运动》，让国际社会了解到这一时期中国华北解放区农村的真实情况。

　　I went to the place where my parents once lived in Shilidian Village. My parents lived and ate with the villagers. During the day, they interviewed one household after another and took pictures. In the evening, they wrote or typed down what they had learned under the kerosene lamp. They actually lived there for eight months, took over 700 pictures and wrote up their findings in two books, *Ten Mile Inn: Revolution in a Chinese Village, and Ten Mile Inn: Mass Movement in a Chinese Village,* telling the world the truth about the rural liberated areas in northern China at the time.

他们到十里店后住在中农王家祥家中，当地人要给我父母开小灶，他们坚决反对，坚持跟当地农民一起吃。他们端着碗到屋外，与村民边吃边聊。如此，当地人不再认为他们是"突然冒出来的外国人"。

They lived at the home of Wang Jiaxiang of Shilidian Village. Some local people proposed to cook exclusively for them, but they firmly declined. They insisted on having the same meal as the villagers. And they took their food outside and chatted with the villagers as they were eating. They were gradually no longer regarded as foreigners by local villagers.

在我父母的旧居，郭锦荣的曾外孙付海保讲道：
In the old residence of my parents, Fu Haibao, Guo Jinrong's great-grand child said,

郭锦荣是我娘的姥姥，住在东屋。柯鲁克夫妇当时就住在这个后堂屋。
Guo Jinrong was my mother's grandma. My great-grandmother lived in this east wide room while they lived in the north room back there.

提到郭锦荣，我母亲讲道：
When talkinig about Guo Jinrong, My mother said,

我记得，当《白毛女》上演的时候，她（郭锦荣）哭了，并说"这就像我的生活"，后来我意识到，苦难有多种，不仅仅是贫穷。
I remember when they showed *Bai Mao Nü (The White Haired Girl)*, Guo cried and said "it's like my life", But I realized afterwards that the poverty is not the only suffering.

这场改革让女人有了土地，有了参与政治、社会活动的权利，有了婚姻自由。在我们翻看的照片上，妇女一边编织，一边参加土改大会。

In this reform women were given land, the right to participate in local politics and social affairs, and the freedom of marriage. The picture in the album that we are looking at shows women were spinning while attending a land reform meeting.

伊莎白回忆过去
Isabel recalling the past

　　我父母在十里店的八个月里，以人类学研究学者的严谨态度，记录下了中国农村的广大农民"实现耕者有其田"的一场社会大变革。

My parents spent eight months in Shilidian Village, upholding their professionalism as anthropologists, they recorded this great reform in China's countryside which gave land to the tiller.

　　八个月后，我父母乘坐根据地唯一的一辆窄轨火车离开了十里店。但是他们并没有登上飞往加拿大的飞机，而是到了一个更偏远、更贫穷的小村庄——河北南海山。

Eight months later, my parents left Shilidian Village by taking the only narrow-gauge train. But they did not take the flight to Canada. Instead, they headed for an even more remote and poor village, Nanhaishan Village of Hebei Province.

1948 年 7 月，我父母意外地收到一份特殊的邀请。从那时开始，他们参与创建了中央外事学校，即北京外国语大学前身。我母亲说：

In July 1948, my parents surprisingly received a special invitation. They took part in establishing the Central Foreign Affairs School, predecessor of the Beijing Foreign Studies University. My mother said,

> 我们在十里店只是旁观者，我们没有参与革命，直到加入学校后，开始领共产党以小米形式发给我们的薪水，我们才真正成为中国革命的参与者。
>
> We were merely observers at Shilidian Village. We didn't fully take part in the revolution until we were asked to teach in the school, receiving millet as our salary paid by the CPC.

1950 年 11 月 21 日，我母亲给她的博士生导师、伦敦政治经济学院的雷蒙德·福斯先生写了一封信。我母亲在信中写道：

On November 21, 1950, Isabel wrote to her doctoral dissertation supervisor, Professor Raymond Firth at London School of Economics and Political Science. My mother wrote in the letter:

> 现在我们越来越被中国发生的巨大变化吸引了。
>
> Now we are increasingly attracted by the great changes in China.

伊莎白的照片

A photo of Isabel

　　2021 年，我母亲已经 106 岁了。她依然住在北京外国语大学的宿舍里，过着简单的生活。

　　My mother celebrated her 106th birthday in 2021. She still lives a simple life on the campus of the Beijing Foreign Studies University.

柯马凯陪他的母亲伊莎白散心

Michael Crook spending his time with his mother Isabel

　　2019 年 9 月 29 日上午，中国国家主席习近平向我母亲颁授 "友谊勋章"。我母亲是 "新中国英语教学的拓荒者"，为中国培养了大量外语人才，为中国教育事业、对外友好交流、促进中国与加拿大民间友好做出了杰出贡献。

On the morning of September 29, 2019, my mother was awarded the Friendship Medal by President Xi Jinping. My mother, a pioneer in English language teaching after the founding of PRC, has helped China train up a great number of foreign language talents, and made outstanding contributions to China's education, international exchanges and people-to-people friendship between China and Canada.

高帆摄影艺术馆馆长高初向柯马凯讲解展品
Gao Chu, the curator of Gao Fan Photography Museum, explaining the exhibits to Michael Crook

高帆摄影艺术馆馆长高初告诉我：
Gao Chu, the curator of Gaofan Photography Museum told me,

这是我们 2011 年 10 月至 2013 年 5 月到伊莎白家中整理出来的卷宗。我们做了 100 多次口述采访，整理了 10 余箱资料。这是"中国摄影史"中重要的一段历史。

From October, 2011 to May, 2013, we visited Isabel Crook at her place and conducted over one hundred interviews with her to obtain these archive materials. We collected more than ten boxes of archive materials which represent an important piece of *The History of Chinese Photography.*

My

Movie

Dream

in

Hengdian,

China

我在中国的电影梦

我出生在刚果（布）的一个大家庭。我的家人来过中国，他们鼓励我去中国看看。

I was born in a big family in Republic of the Congo. Some of my family members had been to China and they encouraged me to visit.

2011 年，我选择到中国浙江省金华市的浙江师范大学学习电影专业。你问我为什么选择这里？因为浙江有一个神奇的地方，那也是我接近梦想的地方——横店。

In 2011, I chose to study movie at Zhejiang Normal University in Jinhua City, Zhejiang Province, China. You ask why I chose this place? Because there is a magical place in Zhejiang, this is also the place where I can pursue my dream: Hengdian.

我在浙江金华生活了近 10 年，学会了汉语，拿到了电影学的硕士学位。2020 年，我还签约了一家当地的传媒公司，成立了"One Man Team"工作室，拍摄一些电视广告。

I have been living in Jinhua, Zhejiang for nearly 10 years. I've learned to speak Chinese and obtained a master's degree in Movie Arts. In 2020, I also signed a contract with a local media company to form a studio named One Man Team to shoot some TVC advertisements.

我努力工作，很努力，但离那个"电影梦"还差得太远。我们都知道，一个人做不了电影。关于电影，我知道得还太少。我渴望了解那个电影梦开始的地方——横店。在这里，我们可以跨越中国的千年。我不想只当个横店的游客，我想在横店当导演，知道更多有关它的故事。

I work hard, really hard, but I still have a long way to go to where I want to be. We all know that one man can't make a movie alone. I know too little about movies. I am eager to know more about the place where my dream started: Hengdian. Here, we can see thousands of years of Chinese history. I don't want to be just a tourist in Hengdian. I want to be a director in Hengdian and know more about its story.

弗洛吉在拍电视广告
Flogy making a TV commercial

我的中国导师余涛教授理解我，他希望有机会帮助我圆梦。

My Chinese supervisor, Professor Yu Tao, understands me, and hopes to help me realize my dream.

俗话说，机会是给有准备的人。我等到了这个机会。我被导师介绍到横店，作为外国人体验横店的拍摄技术。终于，我离电影梦又近了一步。

There is a saying: Opportunity favors only the prepared mind. I waited for this opportunity. I, as a foreigner, was introduced to Hengdian by my supervisor to study movie shooting techniques. Finally, I am one step closer to achieving my dream.

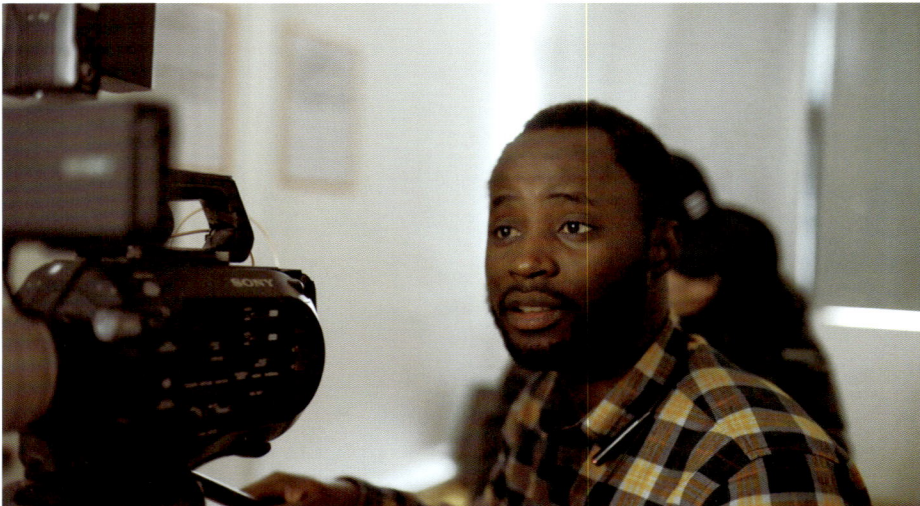

弗洛吉不断努力接近他的电影梦

Flogy keeps trying to get closer to his movie dream

弗洛吉在横店影视城
Flogy at Hengdian World Studios

    深入体验了横店之后，我思考了很多。30 年前，这里只是一个小镇，跟电影没有丝毫关系。然而现在，横店已经成为全球规模最大的影视拍摄基地。为什么？横店是怎样取得如此大的进步的？这个问题一直萦绕在我的心头。

    I thought a lot after observing the movie business in Hengdian. Thirty years ago, this place was just a small town, and had nothing to do with movies. However, Hengdian now has become the world's largest movie and television shooting base. Why? How come Hengdian has made such great progress? This question has been lingering in my mind.

弗洛吉在横店体验虚拟拍摄技术
Flogy experiencing VR shooting technology in Hengdian

弗洛吉与横店集团创始人徐文荣先生交谈
Flogy talking to Xu Wenrong, the founder of Hengdian Group

我渴望知道答案。去拜访横店集团的创始人可能是获取答案的最佳方式。
I need to find the answer. Visiting the founder of Hengdian Group is the best way.

经过一系列的协调，我的请求最终被接受了。
After rounds of communication, my request was finally approved.

　　面对横店集团的创始人徐文荣先生，我非常激动，迫不及待地说出了自己的问题："徐先生，我想知道的第一件事是，横店成功的秘诀是什么？"
　　Meeting up with Mr. Xu Wenrong, the founder of Hengdian Group, I was very excited and couldn't wait to shoot my question, "Mr. Xu, the first thing I would like to know is what's the secret of Hengdian's success?"

秘密？没有秘密的。当然我们先走了一步。横店过去很穷，平均每个人只有三分地，吃不饱，没钱用。怎么带动老百姓富起来？当时想来想去，剩余的劳动力的就业还没解决，应该搞文化产业。这个政府也提出来了，因为拍戏能够带动一大批老百姓致富，所以他们很关心我们的影视基地。政府也成立了机构，自己来管理这个影视基地。政策方面的倾斜、资金的支持、税收的优惠，这些支持对我们很有利。老百姓很高兴，有的当群众演员，有的开小饭店，有的开住宿店……第三产业带动起来。所以慢慢就富起来了。

Secrets? There's no secret. However, Hengdian was a city of trailblazer. Back then, Hengdian was very poor, each person only had a tiny plot of land. People were very poor and starved all the time. How could we solve this problem? At that time, the unemployment rate was high, I thought the cultural industry might be the solution. The government also recommended doing so to improve people's living standards. The government was very supportive of the filming base, and had set up a particular committee. We benefited from the government support, financial backing, and tax benefits. Local people were delighted. Some of them acted as extras, some opened small restaurants, and some opened hotels. Everyone wanted to get involved in the industry, thus the service sector was booming. Therefore, people became richer and richer.

徐文荣先生如是说。
Mr. Xu Wenrong said.

见完了徐文荣先生，我一直在思考，简直停不下来。我打开电脑，给我们国家里我认识的分管电影的领导人写了一封电子邮件，请求视频连线，并把自己的思考告诉他，把横店梦、中国梦是如何实现的告诉他。

After meeting Mr. Xu Wenrong, I couldn't stop thinking. I turned on the computer and wrote an e-mail to the director in charge of cinema in my country, calling for a video conference. I shared my thoughts and described how the dream of Hengdian and the Chinese Dream had been realized.

弗洛吉与刚果（布）电影部部长视频连线
Video link between Flogy and Claver Lembouka Ebenga, Director of Cinema Department of the Ministry of Culture and Arts of the Republic of the Congo

3 个星期后，我的这个请求也被接受了。我想知道，横店（的成功）是否能在我们的国家复制？

Three weeks later, my request was approved. I was wondering whether my country could get some inspiration from Hengdian.

我感觉我的中国电影梦有戏。
I think my Chinese movie dream has a bright future.

中国驻刚果共和国大使馆报道弗洛吉在中国横店的故事

Chinese Embassy in the Republic of the Congo reported Flogy's story in Hengdian, China

✕　　**中国驻刚果共和国大使馆** ＞　　•••

弗洛吉在横店片场交流学习

刚最大私营电视台数字电视台播出画面

CINÉMA

Un Congolais réalise un documentaire sur le centenaire du PCC

Le documentaire du Congolais Flogy Dostov Ngalouo réalisé à l'occasion du centenaire du Parti communiste chinois (PCC) a été diffusé sur Zhejiang TV, l'une des chaînes de télévision chinoises les plus regardées. Il fait découvrir à travers ce documentaire Hengdian, le « Hollywood chinois ».

Il s'agit d'une série de courts métrages documentaires intitulée « 100 ans : l'impression du Zhejiang aux yeux d'étrangers ». L'un des épisodes de ce documentaire est consacré à Flogy Dostov Ngalouo, ce jeune congolais qui travaille comme réalisateur en Chine.

Âgé de 30 ans, Flogy Dostov Ngalouo a découvert sa passion pour le septième art dès son enfance bercée par les films chinois, surtout ceux du Kung Fu. Impulsé par ce rêve cinématographique, il est parti en 2011 du Congo pour étudier à l'université normale de Zhejiang dans la province éponyme, à l'est de la Chine. Après y avoir obtenu une licence en média digital et un master en cinématographie, il fait valoir son talent en travaillant dans une entreprise de média locale en tant que cadreur, monteur et metteur en scène des publicités télévisées.

Désireux de s'approcher davantage de son rêve, Flogy Dostov a eu par l'intermédiaire de son superviseur universitaire la chance de faire une visite de découverte à Hengdian World Studio, surnommé « Hollywood chinois ». Situé juste dans la ville de Jinhua (Zhejiang), où il vit depuis dix ans, Hengdian abrite le plus grand complexe des studios de tournage des films et des séries télévisées du monde entier. Depuis sa fondation en 1996, plus de trois mille équipes de tournage y ont été accueillies avec envi-

Flogy Dostov Ngalouo lors d'un tournage à Hengdian (crédit photo)

ron soixante-dix-mille épisodes de produits audiovisuels tournés, y compris de blockbusters. Pendant son voyage, Flogy s'est émerveillé par la grandeur architecturale des studios qui transportaient les visiteurs à travers le temps. Il s'est imprégné des techniques du tournage en allant sur le plateau, échangeant avec le metteur en scène, l'ingénieur du son et les acteurs et dégustant les technologies pointues telles que la réalité virtuelle.

S'agissant de son inspiration, Flogy a eu le plaisir d'avoir un entretien amical avec le fondateur et ancien président directeur général de Hengdian World Studio, Xu Wenrong, âgé de 86 ans. Ce dernier lui a partagé le secret de la réussite de Hengdian, une localité jadis pauvre. Il s'agit d'un mariage heureux entre l'entreprenariat et le gouvernement : les intrants privés et les mesures de l'État

comme les soutiens finan... et le privilège fiscal ont c... à l'essor des secteurs cu... et cinématographiques, et... conséquent, celui du touris... et de l'hôtellerie. La métamor... phose de Hengdian est un reflet des changements prodigieux qu'a connus la Chine au cours des dernières décennies grâce à la politique d'ouverture et de réforme lancée en 1978. « Hengdian est un modèle inspirant pour le cinéma congolais qui subit un manque criant d'une politique commune pour réveiller son âme qui se trouve actuellement dans un coma profond et pour que les productions des artistes congolais zélés bénéficient d'une plus grande visibilité. Une observation que j'ai partagée avec le ministère de la Culture et des Arts du Congo », a déclaré Flogy Dostov Ngalouo.

Bruno Okokana

The

White

Tea

Blueprint

to

a

Well-off

Life

安吉白茶的扶贫故事

浙江安吉
Anji，Zhejiang

© 殷兴华

安吉白茶技术员向我介绍道：

A white tea planter of Anji County told me,

白茶是叶白脉绿，它中间这根茎脉呈绿色。我们采茶基本上是采一叶一芯，采的时候要这样轻轻地往上提。在市场上，我们这样的茶叶就能卖到高价。

White tea has white leaves with the green vein in the middle. We pick the bud with one leaf, plucking it up gently. This kind of white tea can be sold at a high price in the market.

从 1997 年开始，这里种上了白茶。每年到了三四月份，这里家家户户都开始采茶，这是他们一年收入的重要来源。因为白茶，安吉的这个小村庄成了一个富裕的地方。

White tea has been planted in Anji County since 1997. Every year in March and April, all the families living here begin to harvest tea, which is an important source of income for them. Because of white tea, this small village in Anji has become a wealthy place.

黄杜村党总支书记盛阿伟对我讲：

Sheng Awei, the current Party branch secretary of Huangdu Village, told me,

应该说在 1997 年之前，我们黄杜村还是比较贫穷的，人均收入不足 1000 元。不瞒你说，那个时候有很多姑娘都不愿意嫁到我们黄杜村来，因为很贫穷啊，有很多大龄青年。

Huangdu Village was rather poor before 1997, the per capita income was less than 1,000 *yuan*. To be honest, very few girls wanted to settle down in Huangdu Village, because people here were poor. There were lots of unmarried people in our village.

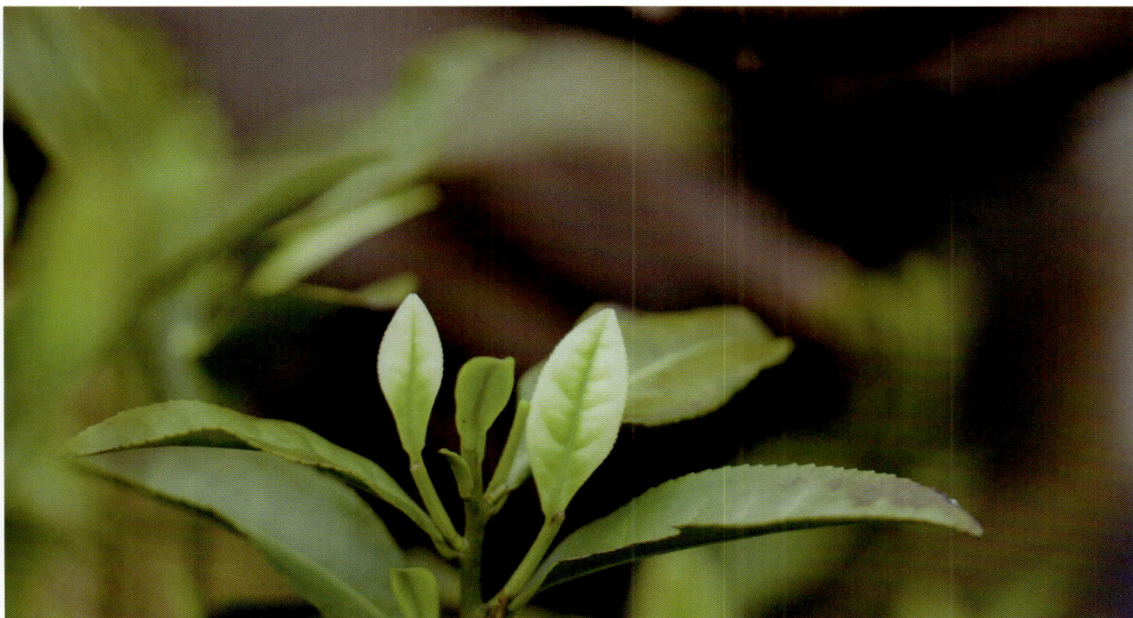

白茶叶白脉绿
White tea has white leaves with the green vein

一位安吉县白茶农户宋昌美也回忆道：
A white tea farmer of Anji County, Song Changmei recalled,

我当时嫁到黄杜村时，其实这是一个比较穷的村。我身边的这些姐妹，我想给她们介绍进来，她们都不愿意进来，说这个村庄穷。

When I got married and settled in Huangdu Village, it was poor back then. I introduced local bachelors to my girl friends, but my girl friends were reluctant to come to this poor village.

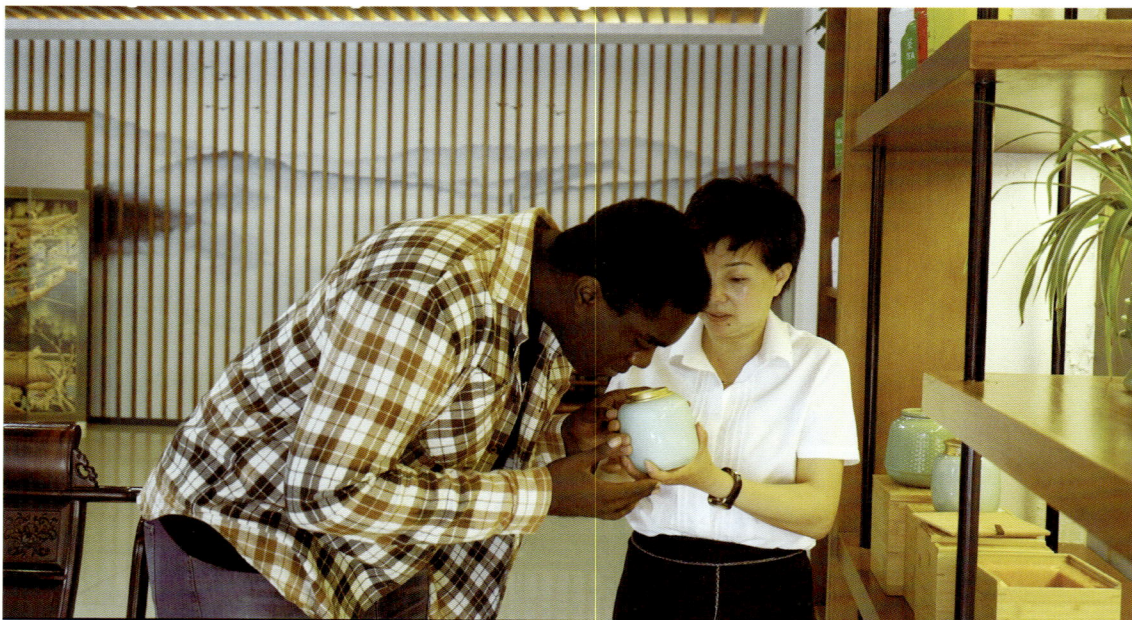

宋昌美带克里象了解白茶

Song Changmei introducing to Christian Zola the white tea

　　黄杜村从 1980 年开始种辣椒，后来种板栗、杨梅、菊花、竹子，什么都种，但是没有找到一条适合黄杜村致富的路。

　　People of Huangdu Village started growing peppers in 1980, then chestnut, waxberry, chrysanthemum, and bamboo. They planted everything, but couldn't figure out the right path for Huangdu village to become wealthy.

盛阿伟对我说道：

Sheng Awei told me，

　　还是要坚持。我们后来种茶叶，坚持下来了，找到了适合自己发展的路。2003年4月9日，时任浙江省委书记习近平同志到我们茶园来调研，我们向他汇报了我们以前特别穷，种白茶以后富起来的经历。习近平同志说："一片叶子富了一方百姓。"

　　Perseverance is a must. We grew tea later and held on to it. Eventually, we found a suitable approach for our own development. On April 9, 2003, Xi Jinping, the then Secretary of the CPC Zhejiang Provincial Committee, inspected our tea gardens. We told him our story of shaking off poverty by growing white tea. Xi Jinping said, "A leaf created an industry and made the local people rich."

他又自豪地说：

He then said proudly，

　　你看这个茶园漂不漂亮，漫山遍野都是白叶一号，都是白茶。这就是我们老百姓致富的茶园基地。

　　Isn't this tea garden beautiful? This garden is filled with white tea called Baiye Yihao. Many tea gardens like this make our villagers rich.

　　关于富裕的秘密，安吉黄杜村村民并没有打算藏起来。他们想把这个致富的秘密分享给大家。

　　As for their affluence, the villagers of Huangdu Village in Anji have no intention of hiding it. In fact, they want to share with others about their path to prosperity.

白茶园前，黄杜村党总支书记盛阿伟与克里象

Sheng Awei, the Party branch secretary of Huangdu Village, and Christian Zola in front of the white tea field

宋昌美说道：

Song Changmei said,

　　那个时候，我也是从电视上看到，说到 2020 年，全国要全面脱贫。当时，我们盛书记号召我们捐赠茶苗。我心里特别高兴，我第一个就举手，表示赞成。既然捐了，那么我们肯定要成功。

　　I once watched on TV that China would lift the whole nation out of poverty by 2020. When our village's Party branch secretary called on us to donate tea seedlings, I was so excited and raised my hands first to show support. Since we decided to donate, we were determined to achieve success.

一片叶子富了一方百姓
A leaf created an industry and made the local people rich

2018 年 4 月，安吉这个村的 20 名党员村民自发地给习近平总书记写了一封信，汇报了村里种植白茶致富的情况，提出捐赠 1500 万株茶苗帮助贫困地区的群众脱贫。

In April 2018, twenty Party members of this village in Anji voluntarily wrote a letter to Xi Jinping, General Secretary of the CPC Central Committee, reporting the village's achievement in growing white tea and offering donating 15 million tea seedlings to poor areas to help lift local people out of poverty.

今年（2021 年）已经是开采种在贵州的白叶一号的第二年了。种下去的茶苗已经有了明显的成果了，弘扬了先富帮后富的精神，对打赢脱贫攻坚战很有意义。

This year (2021) marks the second year that Baiye Yihao has been harvested in Guizhou. The tea seedlings planted have already yielded some results. Those who get rich first help those left behind. It is of great significance to poverty eradication.

在我的国家刚果（金），人们非常喜欢喝茶，但我们的农业还不是很成熟。近几年中国与非洲在农业方面频繁合作，中国为非洲提供种植指导，提高农作水平。

In my country, DR Congo, people love tea, but the agricultural industry in my country is still not well-developed. In recent years, China and Africa have cooperated frequently in the agriculture sector. China has provided Africa with its advanced experience to improve the agriculture in Africa.

我很希望这种通过安吉白茶实现先富帮后富的模式未来可以复制到我的国家，这样会帮助到更多的人。

I really hopes that this model of cultivating white tea to alleviate poverty can be practiced in my country in the future, so as to help more people.

为了亲眼见证"安吉白茶"的扶贫故事，在黄杜村村民的陪同下，我登上了飞往贵州普安县的航班。

In order to know more about how the Anji white tea has facilitated poverty alleviation, I flew to Pu'an County in Guizhou Province accompanied by villagers of Huangdu.

黄杜村向贵州普安县捐赠了 1500 万株茶苗

Huangdu Village donated 15 million tea seedlings to Pu'an County in Guizhou Province

普安的村民热情欢迎克里象
The villagers in Pu'an warmly welcoming Christian

我可以感受到茶叶给这里带来的变化。
I can see how the tea has changed people's lives.

如今的普安相比 3 年前大有不同。
Pu'an has changed greatly in the past three years.

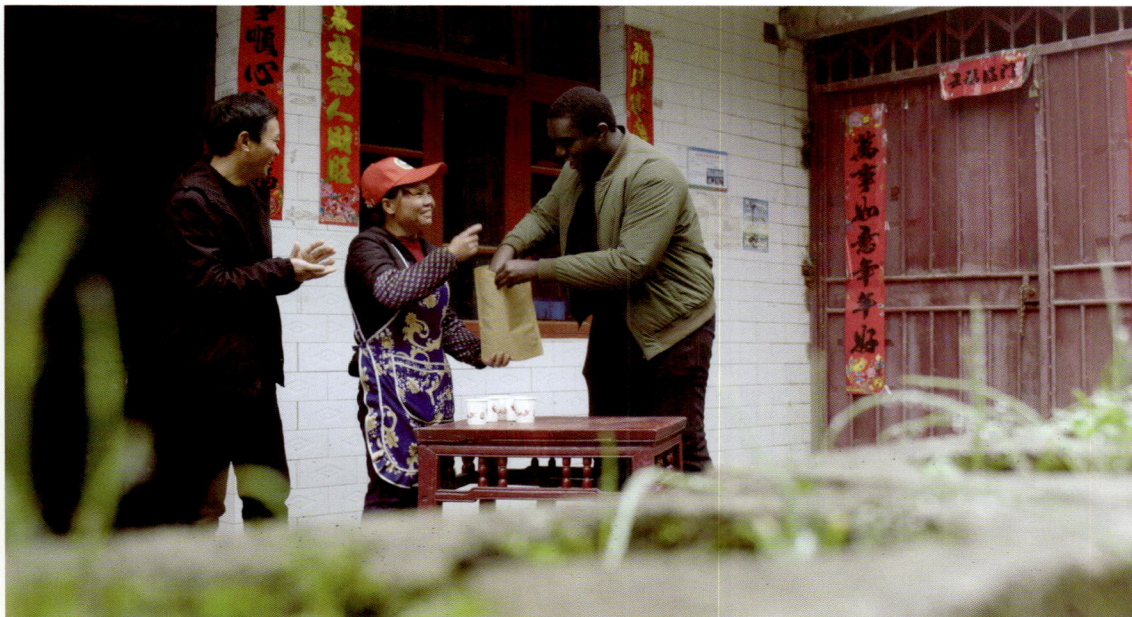

当地茶农喜上眉梢
Local tea farmers are happy

　　我们这个白茶一芽一叶晒干的，要卖到七八百元到一千元一斤。这个是我们自己喝的，要卖三四百元一斤。我们种这个白茶的收入效益，对老百姓肯定是很好啊，很高兴啊。比之前（的生活）好了，很高兴啊。

The white tea picked using "one bud one leaf" technique and allowed to wither and dry in natural sun, can be sold for 1,400 to 2,000 *yuan* per kilogram. The rest of tea can be sold for 600 or 800 *yuan* per kilogram, and we also drink it at home. The economic returns gained from growing white tea have definitely benefited local people. I'm so delighted to see these great changes in our lives!

　　普安县茶农讲到这里，完全抑制不住内心的喜悦，开心地笑了起来。
The tea-planting farmer of Pu'an County told Christian, she laughed with great joy.

The teahouse in Anji County, Zhejiang Province
浙江 安吉 黄杜村茶室

克里象体验白茶的清香
Christian enjoying white tea's fragrant flavor

来一杯吧？
Fancy a cuppa?

这就是关于安吉白茶的故事。喝了白茶，体验了它的香甜，听了白茶的故事，我喜欢上了这里。来一杯吧？

This is the story about Anji white tea. Through tasting the white tea, enjoying its fragrant flavor, and hearing about the stories behind, I have fallen in love with this place. Fancy a cuppa?

The

Clock:

A

Day

and

Night

by

West Lake

西湖十二时辰

辰。
时。

东方明矣，朝既昌矣。——《齐风·鸡鸣》

讲述人：李枝炫
Narrator：Lee Jihyeon

　　李枝炫出生于韩国，现居杭州，自 2017 年起在浙江大学攻读语言学及应用语言学博士学位。来到浙江大学学习后，随着对杭州这座城市的深入了解，她对这座城市的许多地方愈发喜爱，尤其是西湖。西湖给李枝炫的感觉是包容和治愈，所以每当需要放松的时候，她都会去西湖边走一走。

　　Jihyeon was born in the Republic of Korea and now lives in Hangzhou. She has studied for a doctorate in Linguistics and Applied Linguistics at Zhejiang University since 2017. After staying here for a while, with her in-depth understanding of Hangzhou, she became more and more fond of the city, especially West Lake. Jihyeon feels that West Lake is inclusive and healing, so whenever she needs to relax herself, she goes for a walk by the lake.

7:00 a.m. - 9:00 a.m.

李枝炫在西湖边的宝石山

Jihyeon at the Baoshi Mountain by West Lake

西湖处于山岭包围之中，群山峻岭环绕着美丽的西湖，它们像众星捧月一样，捧着西湖这颗江南明珠。

West Lake is surrounded by hills and mountains. Prominent like the moon among the stars, West Lake is a bright pearl of Eastern China resting in the arms of the ridges.

日渐初升，整个杭州开始打破沉寂，早起的市民在西湖边晨跑锻炼，新的一天就这样开始了。

The sun goes up and Hangzhou wakes up to its bustles. The early risers work out by West Lake to start a new day,.

李枝炫品尝奎元馆最著名的美食——片儿川
Jihyeon eating Pian'er Chuan at Kuiyuan Pavilion

　　杭州人最地道的市井早餐往往从一碗面开始。在奎元馆最负盛名的要数"片儿川"和"虾爆鳝面"。瓷碗里盛着的，不仅仅是一碗面，更是老百姓记忆里最杭州的味道。

　　The authentic Hangzhou breakfast begins with a bowl of noodles. The best-known noodles on the menu of Kuiyuan Pavilion restaurant are Pian'er Chuan (noodles served with preserved vegetables, sliced pork, and bamboo shoots) and Xiabaoshan Mian (noodles with fried shrimp and eel), which present the typical Hangzhou flavors loved by the local people.

昔我往矣，杨柳依依。——《小雅·采薇》

巳。
时。

讲述人：骆家婧
Narrator：Jodee Jessica Leigh Lourenssen

　　骆家婧来自加拿大，毕业于加拿大渥太华卡尔顿大学，专业为犯罪学和刑事司法。她于 2018 年来到浙江温州从事英语教学工作，曾多次来杭州游玩。她认为杭州是一个美丽的城市，市民友善，生活充实。

　　Jodee is from Canada. She graduated from Carleton University in Ottawa, Canada, majoring in Criminology and Criminal Justice. In 2018, she came to Wenzhou, Zhejiang Province to teach English. She has visited Hangzhou many times. She thinks Hangzhou is a beautiful city where people are friendly and enjoy a fulfilling life.

9:00 a.m. - 11:00 a.m.

万物生长的西湖初夏

Everything grows in the early summer of West Lake

张岱曾在诗中写道：“日日看西湖，一生看不足。”
Zhang Dai wrote in his poem, "I observe West Lake every day, yet a lifetime is still not enough for this."

骆家婧在西湖畔
Jodee on the shores of West Lake

1954 年，正是在这样美丽的西子湖畔，还诞生了新中国第一部宪法草案初稿。

In 1954, it was by the beautiful West Lake that the first Constitution of the People's Republic of China was drafted.

1972 年，美国总统尼克松在访华时曾赞叹西湖是"美丽的西湖"。

In 1972, the former US president Richard Nixon praised the beauty of West Lake during his historic visit to China.

有句诗是这么写的："槐叶初匀日气凉，葱葱鼠耳翠成双。"西湖的初夏正是万物生长的季节，湖边的树木苍翠茂盛，郁郁葱葱。西湖在每个时节都有不同的美。

A line in a poem describes: "The summer's air is dry and crisp, and the locust trees are covered in lush leaves." In early summer, all lives thrive by West Lake. The trees are exuberant and flourishing. West Lake presents a different type of beauty in each season.

采薇采薇，薇亦柔止。——《小雅·采薇》

午。
时。

讲述人：意涵
Narrator：Ilham Mounssif

意涵生于摩洛哥，后移居于意大利。经浙江省教育厅引进后，意涵目前就职于平阳实验中学。新冠肺炎疫情期间，意涵积极与意大利国家电视台联系，通过多次视频连线分享中国的抗疫经验与真实情况。央视新闻还特别报道了意涵的经历。

Ilham was born in Morocco and later settled in Italy. Introduced by the Department of Education of Zhejiang Province, Ilham is now working in Pingyang Experimental Middle School. During the COVID-19 pandemic, Ilham actively contacted Italian state television and shared China's anti-pandemic experience and real situation through video links. CCTV News also reported Ilham's experience.

11:00 a.m. - 1:00 p.m.

在百年老字号饭店"楼外楼"欣赏西湖美景是个不错的选择

It's a good choice to enjoy the beautiful scenery of West Lake in the century-old brand restaurant Lou Wai Lou

　　在西湖之滨，孤山脚下，有一间百年老字号饭店"楼外楼"，自1848年起，它已接待过海内外多位名人政要，见证了杭州城与西湖的兴衰浮沉。

　　By the shore of West Lake and at the foot of the Gushan hill, sits the Lou Wai Lou restaurant. Since 1848, it has been graced by countless celebrities and important figures. It is a witness of the history of Hangzhou and West Lake.

　　龙井虾仁是富有杭州地方特色的名菜。当年尼克松总统访华时，晚宴的菜单上就有此菜。

　　Longjing Shrimps (Stir-fried Crystal Shrimps with Longjing Tea Leaves) is a typical Hangzhou dish. During Richard Nixon's visit to China, this dish was on the menu at the banquet.

杭州美食：龙井虾仁
Hangzhou cuisine: Longjing Shrimps

　　除此之外的杭州传统佳肴还有西湖莼菜汤和清汤鱼圆。对杭州人来说，它们都是无可替代的家乡食物。

Besides, typical Hangzhou delicacies include Water Shield Soup and Fish Balls Soup. To the Hangzhou locals, they represent an irreplaceable taste of home.

　　赏完西湖美景，在湖边与朋友坐下饮一杯茶，谈天说地，人生快事，莫过于此。

Enjoying the beautiful scenery of West Lake, one can sit down, order a cup of tea, and chat with friends. There is nothing better than this.

申。
时。

讲述人：安娜
Narrator：Rutayisire Mahoro Dianah

　　安娜来自卢旺达，现居杭州，就读于杭州师范大学阿里巴巴商学院，跨境电子商务/国际商务专业。安娜认为杭州是一座美丽而宁静的城市，人杰地灵，风景秀丽。她曾听说杭州被称为一幅画，来了以后深有同感。

Dianah is from Rwanda and now lives in Hangzhou. She is studying at Alibaba Business College of Hangzhou Normal University, majoring in Cross-border E-Commerce/International Business. Dianah thinks Hangzhou is a beautiful and tranquil city with great people and beautiful scenery. She had heard people say that Hangzhou was as beautiful as a painting, and she agreed when seeing it with her own eyes.

3:00 p.m. - 5:00 p.m.

安娜在西湖散步
Dianah rambling at West Lake

2011 年 6 月，"中国杭州西湖文化景观"被正式列入《世界遗产名录》。
In June 2011, West Lake Cultural Landscape of Hangzhou was added to the UNESCO World Heritage List.

与其他的世界文化遗产不同，西湖与杭州城市的关系更为紧密，因此保护好西湖，也始终是杭州的永恒主题。如今，杭州人民像保护自己的眼睛一样，保护着这颗世界的明珠。
Compared with other world heritage sites, what's different about West Lake is its tie to the city of Hangzhou. Therefore, protecting West Lake has been a lasting task for the city. Today, the people of Hangzhou protect this pearl on the earth as they protect their own eyes.

西湖是世界人民的大公园

West Lake is a grand park for all people around the world

从杭州市政府决定实施西湖申遗至今，西湖在不断的修缮整治过程中发生了巨大的变化。杭州市拆掉有碍观瞻的建筑，修复人文景观，保护生态环境……更重要的是，杭州市政府让西湖对所有人免费开放，使西湖成为世界人民的大公园。

Since Hangzhou's Municipal Government decided to apply for nomination in the UNESCO World Heritage List, West Lake has experienced tremendous changes, including renovating facilities, improving scenic spot, and protecting ecological environment. More importantly, West Lake is free for all visitors. It is indeed a grand park for all people around the world.

酉。时。

月出皎兮，佼人僚兮。——《国风·陈风·月出》

讲述人：莫涵熙
Narrator：Camila Bianca Morello

　　莫涵熙来自阿根廷，就读于浙江传媒学院，学习双语播音主持专业。因为对汉语和中国文化非常感兴趣，她在 2018 年来到中国。此外，她还积极在社交媒体上向外国人介绍中国文化。

　　Camila is from Argentina and is studying at Communication University of Zhejiang, majoring in Bilingual Broadcasting and Hosting. Interested in Chinese language and culture, she came to China in 2018. She is also active in introducing Chinese culture to foreigners on social media.

5:00 p.m. - 7:00 p.m.

莫涵熙夜游西湖
Camila's night tour of West Lake

如果说白天西湖显露出她美丽的容貌，那么夜晚她将会述说自己动人的故事。

During daytime, West Lake shows its beautiful visage; at night, it tells its charming stories.

2016 年 G20 峰会上，《最忆是杭州》惊艳了各国领导人。《最忆是杭州》使西湖秀丽的自然风光与浓厚的历史人文交相辉映，呈现出如梦如幻的艺术效果。

During the G20 Summit in 2016, the world leaders were wowed by the show named *The Most Memorable Is Hangzhou*. The show combined the natural beauty and cultural connotation of West Lake, creating a fantastic experience.

西湖如镜，反映着杭州日新月异的变化。如今的西湖开放包容，不断向市民和来客敞开自己的怀抱，并进一步走到全球关注的聚光灯下。

West Lake is a mirror that reflects the changes of Hangzhou. Today, West Lake is open and inclusive. It has opened its arms to the local citizens as well as tourists from afar and has stepped into the spotlight of the world stage.

近年来，杭州不断加快推进城市国际化，朝着建设独特韵味、别样精彩的世界名城的目标载梦前行。G20，西湖开出了一朵灿烂之花；G20 之后，西湖还将继续绽放她的美。

In recent years, Hangzhou is committed to going global and building a world-known city with its unique attractions. Hosting the G20 Summit was a great accomplishment for Hangzhou. West Lake has unfolded many glorious chapters, followed by many more that will be unveiled with time.

既见君子，云胡不喜。——《国风·郑风·风雨》

戌。
时。

讲述人：简
Narrator： Jane Bernadette Garnham

　　简出生在英国，后跟随父母移民至澳大利亚。简于 2019 年来到浙江温州，在一所与澳大利亚本地学校有项目合作的中学，教授英文。简热爱旅行及探索，她受到两位儿子的鼓励，只身来到中国体验全新生活，并选择在此长期居住。未来，她也将继续了解中国，热爱并享受她在中国的生活。

　　Jane was born in the UK and emigrated to Australia with her parents. She came to Wenzhou, Zhejiang Province in 2019 to teach English at a middle school that has a program with a local Australian school. Jane loves travelling and exploring new things. Encouraged by her two sons, she came to China alone to experience a new life and decided to live here for more years. In the future, she will continue to learn about China, and love and enjoy her life in China.

7:00 p.m. - 9:00 p.m.

既见君子，云胡不喜。
——《国风·郑风·风雨》

戌时的钱塘江
Qiantang River from 7 p.m. to 9 p.m.

　　大禹时期之前，杭州曾是一个大海湾。彼时的西湖与钱塘江相连，流着相同的血脉。后来由于泥沙沉积，西湖才逐渐与钱塘江分离。

　　Thousands of years ago, Hangzhou used to be a giant bay. West Lake was once part of the Qiantang River. But due to soil sedimentation, it gradually grew apart.

　　西湖美，美在西湖水。经过多年的发展，治理者们又把钱塘江水再次引入西湖。西湖和钱塘江又一次在这方土地上相拥，杭州也由"西湖时代"迈向"钱塘江时代"。

　　The beauty of West Lake lies in its water. Over time, the water of Qiantang River has been directed back into the Lake, and now they finally reunited. Hangzhou is now moving from the Age of West Lake to the Age of Qiangtang River.

简在钱塘江畔
Jane on the bank of Qiantang River

　　第 19 届亚运会即将来临，杭州还将迎来城市发展的重要时期。相信未来，在杭州参加亚运会的运动员们离开杭州时，想到的不仅仅是奥体的"大小莲花"，还有是西湖这朵灿烂之花。

　　With the 19th Asian Games approaching, the city of Hangzhou will be presented new opportunities for development. In the future, when the athletes leave Hangzhou, they will recall the "lotus" of Hangzhou Olympic Sports Center as well as the gorgeous West Lake.

Live

in

Yiwu

留在义乌

穆德和朋友见面
Moda meeting his friends

锁店老板徐勇军这样评价我：

Xu Yongjun, a business partner of mine said,

我是 2003 年开始跟他做生意的。那时候我们义乌做生意，都是欠一两个月再付钱。开始都害怕，后来他讲信用，我们（的交易额）最多的时候有一两千万元。

I have been doing business with him since 2003. At that time, businessmen always deferred payment for one month or two. Everyone was concerned at first, but Moda always kept his word. Sometimes, the amount of our business deal could reach 10 million to 20 million *yuan*.

穆德和徐勇军聊天
Moda chatting with Xu Yongjun

其实我的生意在 2003 年还经历了一次失败，我当时真的是身无分文。

My business actually failed in 2003, and I was broken at that time.

一个朋友问我，后来怎么重新振作的？

A friend of mine asked me: How did you manage to restart it?

我永不言弃。因为我相信高风险意味着高收益，没有风险也意味着没有收益。我们又回来了。

I never give up. Because I believe that high risk brings high profit. No risk, no profit. And we came back again.

穆德在工作
Moda at work

徐勇军还说：

Xu Yongjun then said,

我们以前做生意都开车跟他去工厂，他不怕辛苦，他是自己下单、接单、验货、装柜。他很勤奋的。

We used to drive with him to the factory. He got invloved in the whole process, including placing orders, receiving orders, examining goods and filling up counters. He is very hardworking.

义乌有无限商机
Yiwu has a great number of opportunities to start business

　　就这样我坚持做了 7 年。生意有了起色，但是我觉得还不够，因为我觉得生意应该转到线上。尽管 2020 年有疫情冲击，但因为我开辟了新的销售渠道，一共出口了价值 1.3 亿美元的商品，营业额没有减少反而增加了。

I have adhered to this habit for 7 years. My business is getting better. But it wasn't enough, I thought I should move the business to the e-commerce platform. Although the pandemic hit the world hard in 2020, I explored new channels to sell commodities. As a result, I exported a total amount of commodities worth of 130 million dollars in 2021 with an increase in the turnover.

义乌市商务局涉外服务中心工作人员每月拜访外商
Staff of Yiwu Municipal Commerce Bureau visit foreign businessmen every month

疫情期间穆德开辟线上销售渠道
During the pandemic, Moda opened up online sales channels

我们去年开始建立这个网站，马上就会投入使用。顾客可以通过这个网页，直接订货。出现了新订单后，我们员工马上跟进，可以减少很多沟通成本。

We set up this platform last year and it will soon be put into use. Customers can place orders on the platform, and our staff can easily track those orders, which greatly facilitate our communication with customers.

我坚持认为互联网是未来的方向，加上这里的政府总是很支持我们。

I always believe that the Internet is the way to go. At the same time, the local government is always willing to support us.

这一天是义乌市商务局涉外服务中心工作人员每月拜访外商的日子。

That day was the day when the staff of Yiwu Municipal Commerce Bureau visit foreign businessmen every month.

义乌市商务局涉外服务中心工作人员告诉我，
The staff of Yiwu Municipal Commerce Bureau told me,

今天过来是想跟你说一声，你被评为了 2020 年度的金牌采购商。
We come here to inform you that you have won award of the Golden Buyer of 2020.

他又说道，
He then said,

听说你去杭州参加活动了。
I heard that you went to Hangzhou to attend an activity.

"对，讲述中国共产党故事。"我说道。
"Yes, to deliver a speech on stories of the CPC," I said.

我喜欢这里，在我心里，感觉这里和约旦是一样的，都是我的家。
I like Yiwu. In my heart, Yiwu is like Jordan. They're both my home.

我爱我家，我爱义乌，我爱"一带一路"。
I love my home. I love Yiwu. I love the "Belt and Road".

现在，我们的产品通过"义新欧"中欧班列，运往俄罗斯、中亚等"一带一路"沿线国家和地区，也通过海运发货到阿尔及利亚、摩洛哥和其他国家。

Now, we send our products to Russia, Central Asia and other countries and regions along the "Belt and Road" by Yiwu-Xinjiang-Europe Freight Train, and ship our products by sea to Algeria, Morocco, and other countries.

穆德在"中国共产党故事的分享会"上讲述自己在义乌做生意的故事
Moda telling his story of doing business in Yiwu at the Sharing Session of Stories of the CPC

穆德在工厂
Moda at the factory

"义新欧"中欧班列
Yiwu-Xinjiang-Europe Freight Train

　　我不禁思索，跟古代丝绸之路相比，我们的商品已经被"义新欧"中欧班列运往了更广阔的世界。这几年来，我们的生意和义乌的经济一起迅速增长，我们都认为义乌是最适合做生意的地方。

Compared with the ancient Silk Road, our goods now could be sent to the whole world by Yiwu-Xinjiang-Europe Freight Train. Our business as well as the economy of Yiwu is growing up fast these years. We all regard Yiwu as the most suitable place for doing business.

　　我想，我留在这里不仅是因为生意，而是我在这里有朋友、有家人，我选择在义乌扎了根。

I think that I live here not just for doing business and making money, but also because this is where my friends and family are.

Remembering

the

Lisbon

Maru

重访 "里斯本丸"

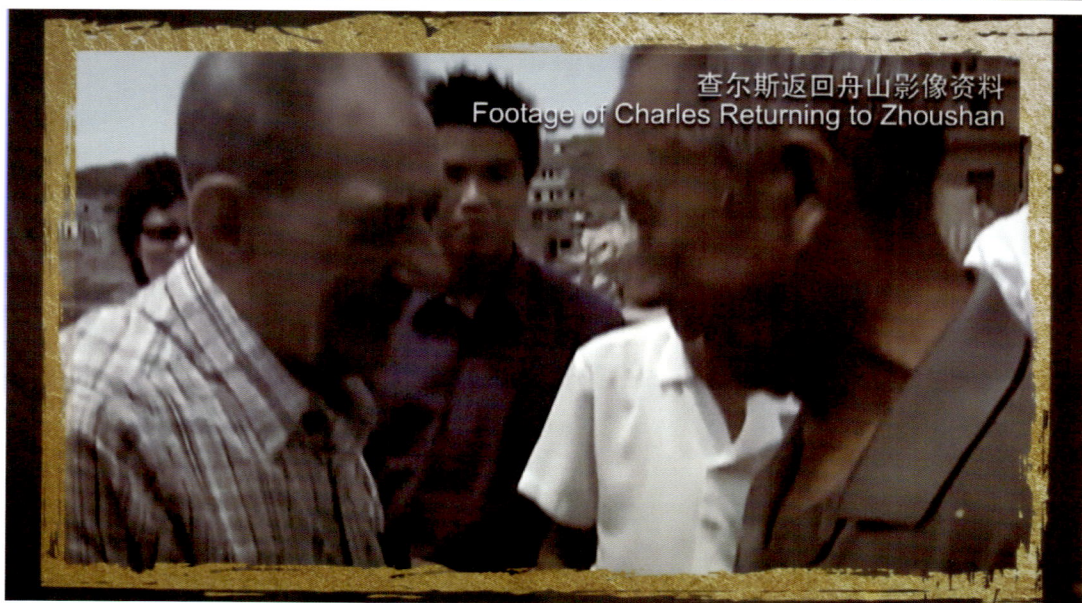

获救 63 年后，查尔斯返回舟山
63 years later after being rescued, Charles returned to Zhoushan

我来自英国，曾在英国学习当代历史与国际政治专业。如今我是浙江工业大学的一位英语老师。在英国的时候，我听朋友说过 70 多年前在美丽的东极岛有一段感人的救援故事，我一直想去考究一下那动人的故事，所以今天我来到了这里。

I come from the UK. I studied Contemporary History and International Politics in the UK. Nowadays, I teach English at Zhejiang University of Technology. When I was in the UK, I heard that more than 70 years ago, a very touching story occurred on Dongji Islands. I have always been longing for knowing more about that story, so today I am here.

我从庙子湖码头登上了东极岛，第一站去了存放 70 多年前那一段历史资料的档案馆——东极历史文化博物馆。这个博物馆有两层，第一层是民风民俗馆，展示的是东极岛渔民旧时期生产、生活、劳动的用具。

I boarded the ferry to Dongji Islands at Miaozihu wharf. The first stop was the Dongji History and Culture Museum, which archives a period of history of more than 70 years ago. The museum has two storeys; the Folk Customs Museum is on the first floor, which exhibits the tools used by the fishermen in the past.

1942 年 10 月 2 日清晨 4 点，一艘日本轮船"里斯本丸"载着 1800 多名英军战俘途经中国舟山东极岛海域，被美国军舰"鲈鱼"号潜艇发射的鱼雷击中。顿时海水涌进船舱，轮船左右摇晃，船上的日本军官和士兵惊慌失措，慌忙逃走。

On October 2, 1942, at 4 o'clock in the morning, a Japanese steamship called *Lisbon Maru* was carrying over 1,800 British prisoners of war (POWs). Passing through the area of Dongji Islands, it was hit by a torpedo launched by the submarine Perch of the US Navy. Suddenly seawater poured into the ship's cabin. The ship swayed from side to side, and the Japanese officers and soldiers on board panicked and fled.

小岛有个好的传统，只要是人命关天的事，不管哪家渔船出了事，大家都会自觉地蜂拥出海相救。那天看到那艘巨轮下沉，肯定有人受伤，每家每户都划着渔船出海救人。当时的渔船很小，一条船最多只能救八个人，小的渔船只能救四五个人。

The islands have a nice tradition. People's lives matter the most, so if one fishing boat had an accident, everyone would rush to lend a helping hand. Seeing such a huge ship sinking that day, those fishermen knew that there would be casualties. Every single household rowed fishing boats to the sea to save people. The fishing boats were very small. Most could only carry up to eight people, while the smaller boats could only carry four or five people.

我看了这些照片以后，真的很难相信军舰爆炸以后还会有人活着。

After looking at these pictures, I find it really hard to believe that people could be alive after the ship exploded.

东极镇文化站站长梁银娣对我讲道：

Liang Yindi, the head of the Dongji Town Cultural Center told me,

因为渔船很小，来不及大批拯救，渔民只能把救上船的英俘尽快运到附近的西福山礁石上，来不及救的英俘被海浪冲走了。总共有46艘渔船出海65船次，就是所有的船都出去了，一直救到海面上没有人了。

Because the fishing boats were too small to carry a large amount of people, the fishermen had to send the British POWs to the nearby Xifushan reef as soon as possible. The British POWs who were not rescued in time were washed away by the waves. In total, 46 fishing boats set sail for 65 times. All the boats went out to save people until no one was left on the water.

村里的渔民真是了不起。

The fishermen in this village are incredible.

"里斯本丸"沉船事件让汤姆难以置信

The shipwreck of the *Lisbon Maru* is unbelievable to Tom

一共有 380 多名英军战俘获救，其余的下落不明，也许是牺牲了。日本军人大部分被他们自救了。这些被救的英军战俘得到了东极岛渔民的照顾，没有衣服穿的，渔民从家中拿出来给他们；没有吃的，渔民即使自己困难也要让他们吃饱。小岛的渔民救援行动很好地诠释了国际人道主义的精神。

More than 380 British POWs were saved, while most of the rest sank to the bottom of the sea. The Japan side saved most of its soldiers. The rescued British POWs were taken care of by the fishermen of Dongji Islands. They had no clothes to wear, so the fishermen got some from their homes. They had nothing to eat, so the fishermen gave them food. The fishermen of the islands vividly demonstrate the spirit of international humanitarianism.

汤姆参观"里斯本丸"模型
Tom visiting the *Lisbon Maru* model

　　在东极岛上，这些精力耗尽的英国战俘终于度过了一个平静舒适的夜晚。然而，第二天日本军人又登上了东极岛，把渔民拯救的英国战俘都抓捕了回去。当时，英国战俘为了不连累岛上的渔民，纷纷主动站了出来，在渔民们感激而又不舍的目光中离开了东极岛。但渔民们还是冒着生命危险救下了三个英国士兵，把他们在青浜岛隐蔽的山洞中藏了五天。

　　Eventually, these exhausted British POWs spent a peaceful and comfortable night on Dongji Islands. However, on the next day, Japanese soldiers landed on the Islands and arrested all the British POWs rescued by fishermen. At that time, in order not to implicate these islanders, the British POWs stood out and left the islands with gratefulness in their minds. However, the fishermen still risked their lives to save three soldiers while hiding them in a secret cave on Qingbang Island for five days.

后来几经辗转，三位英国人被送往了安全区，顺利回到了英国。这才让"里斯本丸"沉船事件和东极岛渔民救人的英雄事迹公之于众，使得战后流落日本的英国战俘通过多种途径回到祖国。

After many twists and turns, the three Britons passed through several safe areas and returned to the UK smoothly. Then the *Lisbon Maru* shipwreck incident and the heroic deeds of fishermen on Dongji Islands went public, which helped the British POWs in Japan return to their motherland.

今天我们在东极岛，浙江的最东边之一，这里也是最早见到太阳的地方。过去的第一缕阳光是一天开始的信号，渔民出海打鱼，岛上的居民种植粮食。而现在当第一缕阳光出现的时候，是岛民迎接第一批来岛上的游客的信号。

Now we are at Dongji Islands, one of the most eastern point of Zhejiang Province. It is also the place which first sees the sun rise in the whole China. In the past, the sunrise means the start of a working day. The fishermen went out for fishing and the people who stayed on the islands planted crops. At present, the sunrise welcomes the first batch of tourists.

救人渔民的后代陈斌，对我讲道：
Chen Bin, the descendant of a fisherman who took part in the rescue activities, said to me,

当时包括我外公在内的好多渔民都参与了那次救援。因为我们岛上的第一个上岛人就是因为船翻掉了，只有他一个人幸存到了我们这个岛上。他上岛以后，每当有大雾的天气，他都会来这里点火，提醒渔民不要在这里触礁。这个岛上的人比较淳朴，有人落水了就一定会把他们救上来。

Many fishermen, including my grandfather, went out to save those soldiers. The first person set foot on our islands because his boat capsized and he managed to get here. Every time when there was thick fog, he would start a fire so as to stop the fishermen from hitting the reef. The islanders are sincere and kind-hearted. They will try their best to save the ones falling into the sea.

东极岛
Dongji Islands

© 舟山市普陀区东极镇

A

Journey

of

Poetry

in

the

Beautiful

New

Countryside

美丽新农村
诗之旅

讲述人：安娜（唐曦兰）
Narrator：Podareva Anastasiia (Ana)

安娜，来自俄罗斯，在浙江学习汉语言文学。她在中国有个好听的名字：唐曦兰。诗人是唐曦兰对自己的定义，写中国诗是她日常最大的爱好。

Ana is from Russia. Now she studies Chinese Language and Literature in Zhejiang. She has a nice Chinese name, Tang Xilan. She defines herself as a poet, and creating Chinese poems is her biggest hobby.

美丽新农村——诗之旅
A Journey of Poetry in the Beautiful New Countryside

我叫 Ana，我有一个好听的中国名字：唐曦兰。我留学杭州，读的是汉语言文学，对中国的诗词抱有浓厚的兴趣。

My name is Ana, and I also have a lovely Chinese name: Tang Xilan. I'm studying in Hangzhou, majoring in Chinese language and literature. I have a keen interest in Chinese poetry.

诗人的情思是在乎山水之间的，遍布风景的浙江就是激发我创作灵感的理想地。

A poet's feelings and thoughts are inspired by mountains and waters. Zhejiang, with her scenic beauty everywhere, is the ideal place which has given me a lot of inspiration.

© 殷兴华

浙江安吉
Anji, Zhejiang

我听说安吉是影片《卧虎藏龙》拍摄地，这里有着美丽的风景、连绵的竹林。带着这份期盼，我来到了安吉，开始了我的美丽乡村之旅。

I have heard that Anji County was once the filming site for the movie *Crouching Tiger, Hidden Dragon* and has the beautiful scenery as well as the Great Bamboo Sea. Excited about seeing it with my own eyes, I went to Anji, and began my journey in this beautiful countryside.

清晨，早起的老伯带我到竹林，教我挖笋。安吉的竹笋是非常有名的，让我迫不及待地想尝试一下。

In the morning, old man rose early to take me into the bamboo forest and taught me how to dig up bamboo shoots. Anji's bamboo shoots are very well known, and I can't wait to try digging them up.

唐曦兰来到安吉寻找创作灵感
Ana visiting Anji for inspiration

我们在这个竹子里面藏着一种很好的酒，又香又甜。
Hidden inside this bamboo is a very tasty wine, sweet and fragrant.

老伯说道。
the old man said.

竹节中有酒！这构思真是太巧妙了！
There's wine in the bamboo. How amazing!

竹笋还是中国佳肴的好原料。新鲜吃，晒干吃，都别有风味。
Bamboo shoots are also a good ingredient for Chinese cuisine. There is always unique flavor whether they are fresh or dried.

竹节中有酒
Wine in the bamboo

走在大竹园村，大竹园村村委工作人员向我介绍道：
Walking in Dazhuyuan Village, the village committee staff of Dazhuyuan Village introduced to me:

这里也是一片竹园。这个地理位置特别低，下雨的时候农户家里面就容易进水。其实我们在前期规划的时候就考虑到，既把村庄变美，又把民生问题解决掉。
Here is another bamboo field. The terrain here is particularly low. When it rained, water used to get into the farmhouses easily. We took that into consideration in our early planning, to make the village beautiful and at the same time, to solve the villager's livelihood problems.

我想这就是当地人的智慧，尊重自然，融于自然。
I think it is the wisdom of the local people, to respect nature and to blend in.

大竹园村会呼吸的地

The breathing land in Dazhuyuan Village

我的诗的第一句就这样产生了："竹林翠韵酒肴鲜。"

The first line of my poem came naturally: "The farm wine and food smell as fresh as the country greeneries."

当地人告诉我，安吉的观光小火车也是个有意思的设计，它的轨迹环绕了18 个不同的家庭农场。看着远处缓缓而来的旅游小火车，我等不及要去体验一下。

Local people told me that the mini tourist train in Anji is also a cute design, and its track circles 18 different family farms. Seeing the mini tourist train slowly approaching, I can't wait to take a ride.

鲁家村小火车地图
Lujiacun Village mini-train map

鲁家村党委书记朱仁彬对我说：
Zhu Renbin, the Party branch secretary of Lujiacun Village, told me:

小火车是鲁家村的交通代步工具，去美丽乡村旅游的人，他首先脑子里就会想到，鲁家（村）挺好的，有小火车。

The mini-train is the public transportation of Lujiacun Village. If you want to tour the beautiful countryside, the first thing that comes to your mind is the mini-train of Lujiacun Village.

鲁家村党委书记朱仁彬同唐曦兰在小火车上聊天

Zhu Renbin, the Party branch secretary of Lujiacun Village, chatting with Ana on the mini-train

鲁家（村）在发展的时候搞农场的原因，也是让农民富起来。既让人留在家里面把家照顾好了，也让他们的收入提高了。农民的小洋房盖起来了，小别墅也盖起来了。我们有些外国友人也说，很美慕我们鲁家（村）的村民，也想做鲁家（村）的村民。听了这样的话我挺开心的。

The reason they set up these farms is to help the farmers get rich to enable them to stay at home and take care of their families while making more money. They built up their houses and their villas. Some foreign friends said that they envied us villagers and wanted to be one of us. Hearing this, I'm very happy.

回乡创业的青年民宿主对我说道：

The B&B owner who returned to hometown said to me,

　　最主要是我们这边整体的大环境也很好，有山有水有田地。我自己也是在外面上班，然后开民宿。现在自己的家乡发展得这么好，游客也比较多，所以觉得还是回家比较好。

The most important is that the environment here is great, with mountains, waters and fields. I worked outside and then ran a B&B in the hometown. Many tourists come here because of the development of the hometown. So it's better to come back.

美丽乡村在年轻人和乡贤的带动下，经济更具活力。第二句诗自然而然地飘入我的脑海："景美村幽恰自然。"

The beautiful countryside has a more dynamic economy driven by young people and local sages, so the second line of the poem naturally floated into my mind: "And the quiet village best matches the beautiful sceneries."

余村，安吉另一个有特色的村庄，如今因绿水青山而闻名，数字赋能更推进了当地的经济发展。

Yucun Village is another distinctive village in Anji. Now it's prestigious for its lucid waters and lush mountains. And the digital technology has advanced the local economy even further.

安吉余村
Yucun Village in Anji

余村以绿水青山闻名遐迩
Yucun Village is famous for its lucid waters and lush mountains

余村党支部副书记俞小平介绍道：
Yu Xiaoping, the Party branch deputy secretary of Yucun Village, said:

这是一个我们的智慧农业系统，它可以显示风向、风速、空气，包括土壤的湿度。像病虫害监测就用无人机，它就会精细化地喷洒农药，减少农药的使用量。对我们起的保护生态的作用非常好。

This is our smart farming monitoring system. It can display the wind direction and speed as well as the humidity of air and soil. And for pest monitoring, we used UAVs to carry out accurate spraying of pesticides, so as to reduce the amount of pesticides to be used. That's really helpful.

余村的智慧农业系统
Smart farming monitoring system in Yucun Village

　　每个村庄都有自己的"数字赋能"故事：在大竹园村，浙农码会显示你这个白茶在哪个区域（采摘）的；鲁家村建立了一个完整的大数据区块链，今天来了多少游客，通过大数据也可以管控得了。数字赋能已经深入到了浙江美丽乡村建设的方方面面。

　　It seems that every village has its stories of Digital Empowerment: in Dazhuyuan Village, agricultural QR code will show you where the white tea is produced; Lujiacun Village has set up a complete big data blockchain that can show us how many tourists have come today with this big data technology. Digital Empowerment has penetrated into every aspect of the construction of beautiful countryside in Zhejiang.

绿水青山就是金山银山

Lucid waters and lush mountains are invaluable assets

我想把这个科技元素也融入我的诗里："智赋新农贤雨聚。"

I wanted to incorporate this technological element into my poem as well: "A new pool of digital talents gathered to help farm households."

这是绿水青山被赋予新的价值的秘诀，是值得吟诗歌颂的。绿水青山就是金山银山。

It shows how the lucid waters and lush mountains are endowed with new values, which is worth praising. Lucid waters and lush mountains are invaluable assets.

竹林翠韵酒肴鲜
景美村幽恰自然
智赋新农贤雨聚
青峦碧水育金山
唐曦兰

唐曦兰的诗
Ana's poem

古往今来，文人墨客们对这绿水青山留下过多少文字和诗篇。我再次被眼前的宁静和谐的景象感染了。

Throughout the ages, poets have written endless words about these lucid waters and lush mountains. Such a peaceful view has greatly inspired me again.

我亲身体会了人们内心的幸福、喜悦和安宁。安吉只是浙江美丽新农村里的其中一个，我在浙江的寻诗之旅，才刚刚开始……

I experienced other people's happiness, joy and peace of mind. Anji County is just a small part of Zhejiang's beautiful new countryside, and my journey has just started.

During

2020—2021

I

was

in

Wenzhou

我在 温州 这一年

辛成乐参加全国抗击新冠肺炎疫情表彰大会
Brett attending the national meeting which commended role models in China's fight against the COVID-19 pandemic

从小时候起，我就一直想成为一名医生。我经常照顾我的祖母，她年老时生了很重的病，在床上突发心脏病，那时候我还很小，就在祖母旁边，但我不知道怎么做心肺复苏术。这坚定了我实现梦想的计划，我满怀信心来到中国，以寻求更多学习机会。我完成了我的外科医学学业，并且获得省级奖学金以攻读儿科医学硕士。

When I was a kid, I always wanted to be a doctor. I often took care of my grandmother, who was seriously ill in her old age. She had a heart attack when I was quite young. I was then right next to her, but I did not know how to do CPR. Since then, I was determined to pursue my doctor dream. I came to China with great confidence to look for more opportunities. I successfully got my Bachelor of Medicine and Surgery degree. I have also obtained a provincial scholarship to pursue the master's degree of medicine in pediatrics.

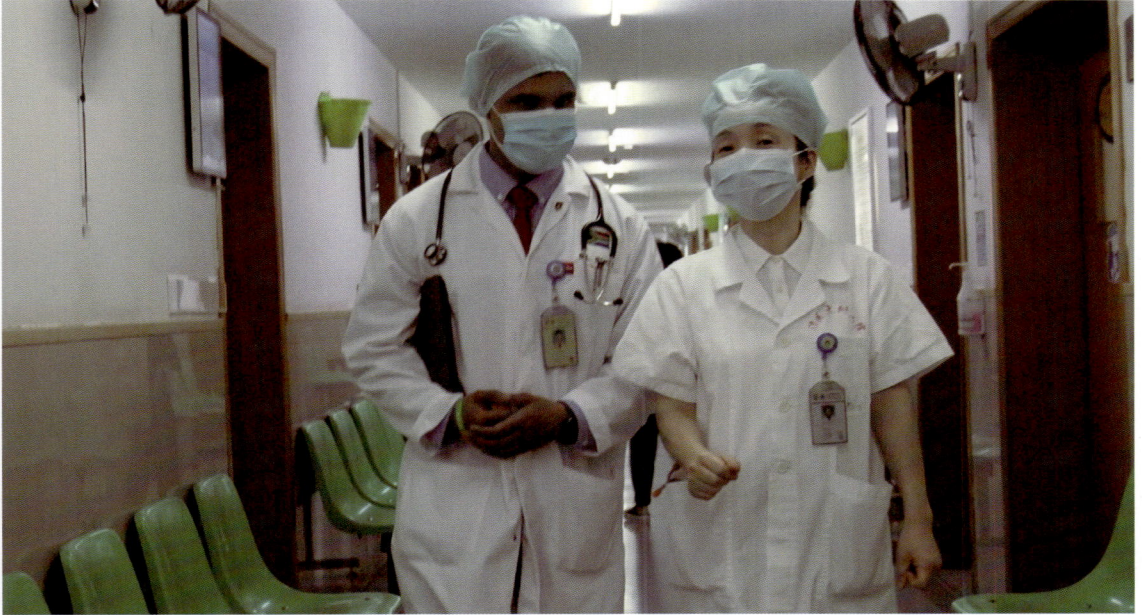

辛成乐（左）在医院工作
Brett (left) working in the hospital

　　毕业那年，我在温州医科大学附属第二医院及育英儿童医院实习。不寻常的事情发生了，新冠肺炎疫情在全世界大暴发。

　　In the last year of my study, I was on my internship at the 2nd Affiliated Hospital and Yuying Children's Hospital of Wenzhou Medical University. Something unusual happened at that year: the COVID-19 pandemic spread across the world.

　　我的妈妈和爸爸很担心我。在 2020 年年初新冠肺炎疫情期间，温州是除了湖北省之外受关注的地区之一。

　　My mom and dad were quite worried about me. During the COVID-19 pandemic at the beginning of 2020, Wenzhou was one of the hotspots besides Hubei Province.

三周内，他们能够控制新冠肺炎疫情。我认为这些努力卓有成效，而且我也能从中学习控制以及预防方法去对抗新冠肺炎疫情。

The spread of COVID-19 pandemic was put under control within three weeks. That was very effective, and I was also able to learn about the controlling methods, as well as the preventive measures against COVID-19.

2020 年 2 月至 5 月，我作为一名医生志愿者，与温州一起度过了那段艰难的时光。我的团队帮助我制作了内容丰富的视频，介绍了有关新冠病毒的感染、疾病、流行病学、发病机理、控制、预防措施以及治疗手段。

During February 2020 to May 2020, I played my part as a volunteer doctor to help Wenzhou during that tough time. My team helped me produce informative videos to introduce the infection, disease, epidemiology, pathogenesis, control, preventive measures and treatment of COVID-19.

我的研究生导师蔡晓红说道：

Cai Xiaohong, my supervisor said,

当时我确实在一线工作。出现疫情之后，我们温医大附二院的儿科第一时间成立了儿童疫区发热门诊，设计了一套发热儿童从就诊到疑似病例隔离，这么一个闭环式运行体系。整个疫情期间，没有出现过一个漏诊的病例。阿乐是我的硕士研究生，他就和我们一起把我们医院，还有温州疫情防控的真实情况，好的抗疫经验拍成视频，传到了国内外的社交平台上。

I worked at the front line of fighting against the pandemic at that time. After the pandemic emerged, the department of pediatrics of the 2nd Affiliated Hospital of Wenzhou Medical University established a fever clinic for children at once. We have designed a closed-loop system from medical consultation to patient isolation. None of the COVID-19 case was missed out during the pandemic. I'm the supervisor of Brett's graduate program. He made videos with us on successful anti-pandemic practices and efforts in pandemic control of our hospital and Wenzhou and uploaded them to social platforms at home and abroad.

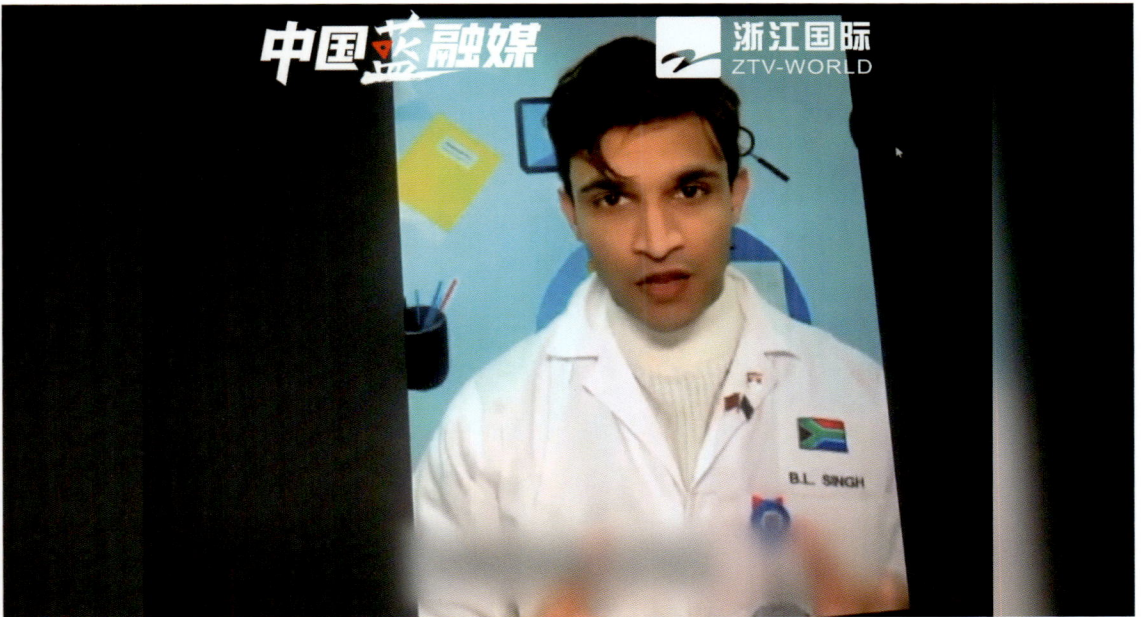

辛成乐发布了一系列抗疫视频

Brett released a series of anti-pandemic videos

我的选修课和实习是在澳大利亚、南非和中国的医院里完成的。

I have completed my electives and internships in hospitals in Australia, South Africa and China.

我见识了不同的卫生治理方法和不同的医疗保健服务，中国医学界一切都富有行动力，而非是空谈。

I have got to know different methods of Health Governance and Health Care Service Delivery. There is a strong drive for research and development in Medical Science in China. It's all action and no empty talk.

辛成乐（左）与导师蔡晓红（右）
Brett (left) and his supervisor Cai Xiaohong (right)

辛成乐与朋友在热烈讨论

Brett having a heated discussion with his friend

　　我在大学的时候有机会参加了许多科技创业竞赛来锻炼我自己。在浙江"互联网＋"大赛中，一位评委启发了我。他建议我把我的儿科研究和一个可扩展的业务模型融合起来。

　　When I was in university, I participated in many technology entrepreneurship competitions, and I was inspired by one of the judges of the Internet Plus competition of Zhejiang. He told me to marry my pediatric research and a scalable business model.

温州医科大学国际教育学院院长金利泰说道：

Jin Litai, dean of School of International Education of Wenzhou Medical University said,

　　阿乐在温州待得时间久了，所以也受到这里氛围的感染，一直有创业的想法。对于他这种情况，我们学校也是有一定支持的。比如在实验场地、技术指导还有创业培训等方面。到了 2020 年 5 月，我们国内的疫情基本上问题不大了，但是阿乐的老家，南非，疫情越来越严重。我们学校帮他联系了一个国内做公益的组织，通过他也给南非邮寄了好几批口罩之类的防护用品。

　　Brett has been living in Wenzhou for a long time. He is influenced by the entrepreneurship atmosphere here for starting a business. In this case, our university offers support, such as providing experiment sites, technical guidance, and entrepreneurship training. The domestic pandemic has been put under control in last May. Nevertheless, in Brett's hometown, South Africa, the stuation was getting worse. Our university contacted a charity organization to donate masks and other materials to South Africa.

　　中国有 14 亿多人口，56 个民族。非洲也有 12 亿人口，它的目标是在未来 25 年内增长到 20 亿人口。这是预期人口增长最快的地方，希望我们可以参加中非医疗合作高级会议。

China has a population of 1.4 billion people and of 56 ethnic groups. Africa has a population of 1.2 billion and aims to increase to 2 billion in the next 25 years. "Africa has the fastest expected population growth and we hope to attend the High-Level Meeting on China-Africa Health Cooperation.

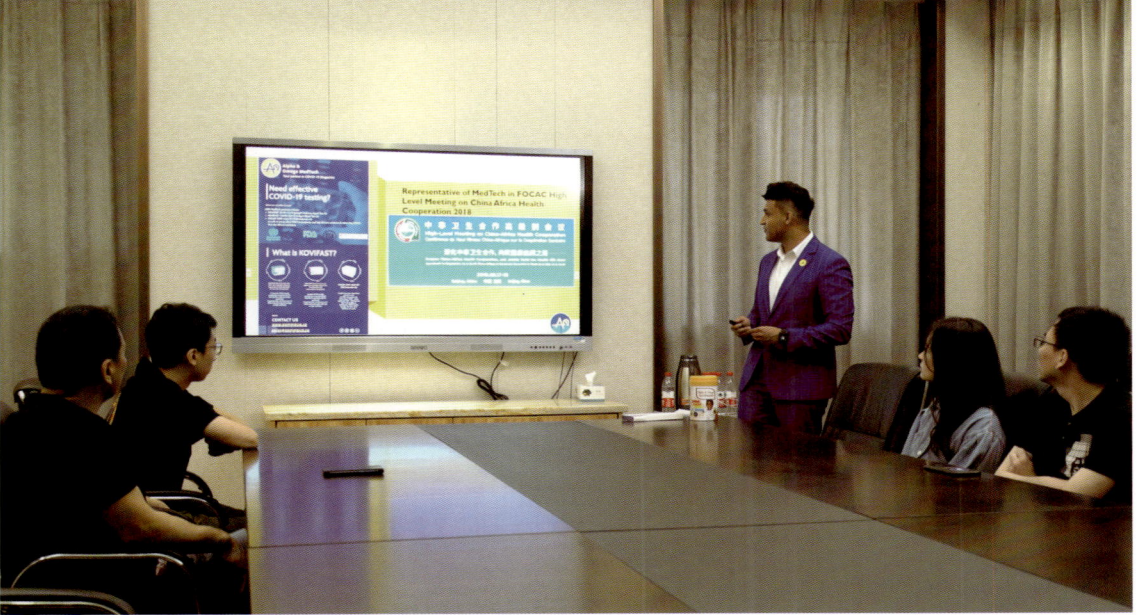

辛成乐希望可以参加中非医疗合作高级会议

Brett hopes to attend the High-Level Meeting on China-Africa Health Cooperation

2021 年是我在中国的第十年。我相信我已经成为一个新温州人。温州是企业家和敢于开拓国外市场之人的家园，他们勇于创新，也满怀对团体的爱，他们敢为人先，也见证着中国经济的飞速发展。

The year of 2021 marks the 10th year of my stay in China. I believe that I have become a new Wenzhounese. Wenzhou is the home of entrepreneurs and those who spearhead in expanding international market. They have innovative spirit and deep love for the community. They have the courage to take the lead and witness the rapid development of China's economy.

辛成乐原意用生命来实现远大目标
Brett willing to invest his life to reach his big goal

温州医科大学
Wenzhou Medical University

　　中国帮助我建立了良好的职业道德、道德实践以及强大的竞争力。我希望运用这些技能，改善非洲的医疗服务，并促进当地科技进步。并让年轻科学家，拥有他们所需要的设备，我也愿意用我的生命来实现这个目标。

China has helped me to build good work ethics, moral practice, and great competitiveness. I hope to use these skills to improve health care service delivery in Africa, and to promote local scientific and technical progress to equip young scientists with the tools they need, and I am also willing to invest my life to reach this goal.

王力、范德维和欧德三人正在下棋聊天
Alex, Michael, and Allan, playing chess and chatting

"来中国后，什么事情印象最深刻？"欧德说问道。

"What impressed you most after coming to China?" Allan asked.

"快递。" 范德维说。

"Express delivery," Michael said.

"我觉得是外卖。"王力回答道。

"For me, it's gonna be take-out," Alex said.

"我印象最深的是移动支付。"欧德说道。

"For me, it's mobile phone payment," Allan said.

除了这些，"浙"里还有其他因为数字赋能而产生的有趣故事。

Besides, there are many interesting stories about smart Zhejiang empowered by digitalization.

三人分享自己的经历

The three of them shared their experiences

讲述人：王力
Narrator：Van Aleks

　　王力出生于俄罗斯，后移居美国。他自幼学习汉语，热爱中国文化。顺利通过 HSK（中国汉语水平考试）六级考试后，他进入浙江大学控制科学与工程学院学习。

　　Van Aleks was born in Russia and later moved to the United States. He has learned Chinese since childhood and ardently loves Chinese culture. After successfully passing HSK level 6, he entered College of Control Science and Engineering, Zhejiang University.

电子商务，也就是在互联网上做生意，现在变得越来越受欢迎了。而我所在的这座城市，是中国的电子商务之都。现在，电子商务有了更高阶的产业形态，直播带货。

E-commerce, which refers to doing business through the Internet, is getting more popular nowadays. The city where I live is the city of e-commerce in China. Now the e-commerce has evolved to a new form of business. It's called livestreaming commerce.

在杭州有很多产业园都是专门从事直播带货的。各有特色的主播们在网络平台上开直播卖产品，有些厉害的主播介绍完商品后，只需要几秒，存货就全部售罄了。

Many industrial parks in Hangzhou are specialized in livestreaming promotions. Streamers on diverse social media platforms conduct livestreams and sell products. For those popular streamers, after introducing their products, they could run out of stock in few seconds.

我简直不敢相信这样的销售速度。

I can't believe that sales speed.

主播大利对我说，最厉害的就是"三、二、一，上链接"就没有了，就那个链接一亮起来马上就没有了，这种情况是经常会发生的。

Dali, a streamer told me, what's awesome about the livestreaming is that when the streamer says "three, two, one, hit the link" and the products could be instantly sold out before the words were out of mouth. This situation happens very often.

开一个直播账号就能卖东西，就能赚到钱？事情一定没有想象的那么简单。每个行业都有二八现象，而成为那 20% 也没有那么简单。

Does it mean that opening a livestreaming account is all we need to sell products and make money? The truth is much complicated than it looks like. The Pareto principle also applies to the livestreaming industry. Only the best of the best can be the vital few.

王力参观电商品牌的直播间
Alex visiting the livestreaming room of E-commerce Brands

主播雪宝告诉我：
Streamer Xuebao said to me,

　　首先，我觉得成为头部主播必须十分努力。因为主播这个行业更新迭代非常快速，淘汰率也非常高，想让粉丝一直信任你、喜欢你、来看你，那首先得站在他们的角度去思考问题，提供最优的服务还有最低的价格，长此以往他们就会非常信任我。

　　I think hard-working is a must for those who want to be top streamers. The livestreaming industry changes and upgrades very fast. The competition in the market is fierce. If you want your followers to like you, trust you, and watch your livestreaming, you should first put yourself in their shoes, and provide them with the best service at the lowest price. In the long run, they will build trust in you.

主播雪宝和王力聊天
Streamer Xuebao chatting with Alex

主播大利告诉我：
Streamer Dali said to me,

我来浙江是因为我想做电商，我必须来杭州，杭州这边它有很完整的产业链，比如我想要个好的食品，我想要漂亮的饰品，我第二天就能联系到它的商家源头。

I come to Zhejiang because I want to start e-commerce business. There is an integrated industrial chain in Hangzhou. For example, if I want to find some good food or beautiful accessories, I can find the original merchants the next day.

个人魅力、产业链当然重要，而地方政府的服务配套更是必要。
The streamer's charming personality and integrated supply chains are important, while the supporting services of local government are also indispensable.

浙江乌镇
Wuzhen, Zhejiang

　　小桥流水人家，这大概就是外国人对中国水乡生活的一种印象。然而乌镇不止有美景，它还是世界互联网大会的永久举办地。每年来自全世界的 IT 领军人物们都会到这里讨论数字化发展的前景。

　　The foreigners' impression on water towns in China are composed of small bridges, flowing water and small households. However, apart from its beautiful scenery, Wuzhen is also the permanent venue of the World Internet Conference. Every year, leaders and tycoons in the IT industry from all over the world will come here and discuss about the development prospect of digitalization.

乌镇是外国人眼中的江南水乡
Wuzhen is a water town in the eyes of foreigners

欧德想在乌镇寻找答案
Allan trying to find answers in Wuzhen

江南水乡和互联网，它们是怎么发生化学反应的呢？先让我带你们逛逛乌镇，感受下这里的"黑科技"。

Water town and Internet, what is the chemistry behind these two things? Let me first show you around to have a glimpse of the cool tech here.

乌镇当地人每天就生活在这样的数字赋能里。乌镇为什么会和互联网深深地捆绑在一起呢？我想从当地人那边寻找答案。

Every day, the local people lead easy and comfortable lives empowered by digital technology. Why Wuzhen is closely connected with the Internet? I attempted to get the answer from the local people.

一个小女孩说道：
A little girl living in Wuzhen said,

因为这边的美景特别的好看，而且街道特别干净。还有这边的人们特别聪明。
Because the scenery is very beautiful, the streets are very clean, and the people here are wise.

一位乌镇居民说道：
A resident of Wuzhen said,

因为我们乌镇它保留了很多老建筑，同时出了很多名人。
A large number of old buildings are well-preserved in Wuzhen, and it is closely bound with many great names.

一位老人说道：
An old person said,

本来这个房子有三百多年了，本来很破的，我们修不起，现在开发得就是很好很好。
This house has a history of over 300 years. It used to be dilapidated because we couldn't afford its maintenance, but now it is wellrefurbished.

一位年轻的女士回答道：
A young lady working in Wuzhen replied,

我觉得互联网是一个非常重要的一个原因，乌镇也是互联网大会的举办地。所以其实我们也是享受到第一波的红利，更多地通过网络的平台（宣传乌镇）可以让乌镇变得更好，让更多的人知道。
I think Internet has played a significant role in these changes. Wuzhen is the permanent venue of the World Internet Conference, and we have benefited a lot from the progress. By promoting Wuzhen through the Internet, more people will get to know this place and help make it better.

欧德从当地人那边寻找答案

Allan attempting to get the answer from the local people of Wuzhen

欧德从当地人那边寻找答案

Allan attempting to get the answer from the local people of Wuzhen

乌镇作为"世界互联网小镇"，到处都是"黑科技"

As a "World Internet town", Wuzhen is full of cool tech

世界互联网大会的永久举办地
The permanent venue of the World Internet Conference

自从乌镇成为世界互联网大会的永久举办地，乌镇已经不只是个江南小镇，而是"旅游小镇""戏剧小镇""世界互联网小镇"。

After Wuzhen became the permanent venue of the World Internet Conference, it has transformed from a small water town to a tourist town, a drama town, and the World Internet town.

乌镇的发展奇迹是中国经济发展的奇迹。

Wuzhen's development is an epitome of China's rapid economic development.

范德维在"鱼菜共生"系统中捞鱼
Michael fishing in the "aquaponics" system

在中文里 aquaponics 被称为"鱼菜共生",意为鱼和蔬菜和谐共生。
In Chinese, "aquaponics" is called Yu Cai Gong Sheng, which refers to the harmonious co-existence of fish and vegetable.

水是从鱼池过来的水,它就是起到一个吸收养分又能够过滤水质的一个作用,然后通过另外一端水又回到这个鱼池,是一个循环。
The water in this pool comes from the fishpond over there. It could absorb the nutrients in the water and remove impurities, and then filter the water back into the fishpond through the other end. It is a whole circulation.

"鱼菜共生"系统种出的蔬菜十分可口
The vegetables grown by the "aquaponics" system are very delicious

现在的"鱼菜共生"融合了种植、养殖、微生物、物联网、大数据等技术。因为这样的技术运用，这里的鱼先生和菜小姐特别受欢迎。

The model of aquaponics integrates elements such as agriculture, aquaculture, microbiology, IOT and big data. Thanks to these techniques, Mr. Fish and Mrs. Vegetable have become quite popular.

数字赋能同样也藏在这一排排的玻璃阳光房。
Digital technologies have also been implemented in these greenhouses.

德清智能节水灌溉示范园负责人介绍道：

A director of Deqing Intelligent Water Saving Irrigation Demonstration Park said,

我们目前总共是 5 个人，负责我们整个 400 亩的园区的管理，因为我们主要依靠设备和智能技术进行灌溉，所以我们人工不需要太多地进行干预。

Now we have only 5 people taking care of the entire zone of about 27 hectares. We mainly rely on devices and smart technology for irrigation, so little manual labor is involved.

5G 和物联网技术与分布在各板块的数百个传感器连接，对植物的用水情况可以进行实时感知和精准计量。通过"大数据 +"的监管，乡村建设里的垃圾分类也做得很有效果。每个垃圾桶上都有二维码芯片，自动垃圾车有 GPS 定位等等。由于数字工具的使用，浙江的乡村正变得愈发高效和美丽，供所有人享受。

The technologies of 5G and IOT are connected with hundreds of sensors distributed in different sections to detect and measure the volume of irrigation water for the plants on a real-time and accurate basis. Digital facilities are used to improve every aspect of the village with the Big Data Plus framework. For example, each garbage bin has a QR code, while automatic garbage trucks are equipped with GPS. The digital facilities have made every village in Zhejiang more efficient and beautiful, which can benefit all people.

在中国总能体验到一些有意思的事。

There's always something new to experience in China.

园区内通过智能设备提高效率

Improving efficiency through intelligent devices in the zone

《100 年·外国人眼中的中国浙江记忆》2021 年 7 月 1 日正式开播。

100 Years: The Impressions of Zhejiang, China in Foreigners' Eyes was officially launched on July 1, 2021.

近 20 位世界各地的外国友人参与节目创制，从国际传播视角，探寻从 1921 年到 2021 年，中国共产党建党百年的历史征程。

About 20 foreign friends from all over the world participated in the program production. The program focuses on the achievements made under the leadership of the CPC from 1921 to 2021, and presents the history of the CPC from the perspective of international communication.

节目播出后，上线超百家新媒体平台，节目点击量和话题数双双破亿。

After the program was broadcasted on over one hundred media platforms, the view and hashtag number of the program have respectively exceeded over 100 million.

中国驻刚果共和国大使和约旦驻华大使致信表示肯定和感谢。

This program has received high praise from the Chinese Ambassador to the Republic of the Congo and the Jordanian Ambassador to China.

这个系列的节目选题，覆盖红色奋斗故事、中国的改革创业故事、中外文化交流故事，以及中国的伟大成就故事。更多关于中国和中国共产党的故事，尽在《100 年·外国人眼中的中国浙江记忆》节目。

This series of this program covers the stories ranging from the development of the CPC, the reform and entrepreneurship in China, the cultural exchanges between China and other countries, and the great achievements of China. More stories about China and the CPC can be found in the program of *100 Years: The Impressions of Zhejiang, China in Foreigners' Eyes.*

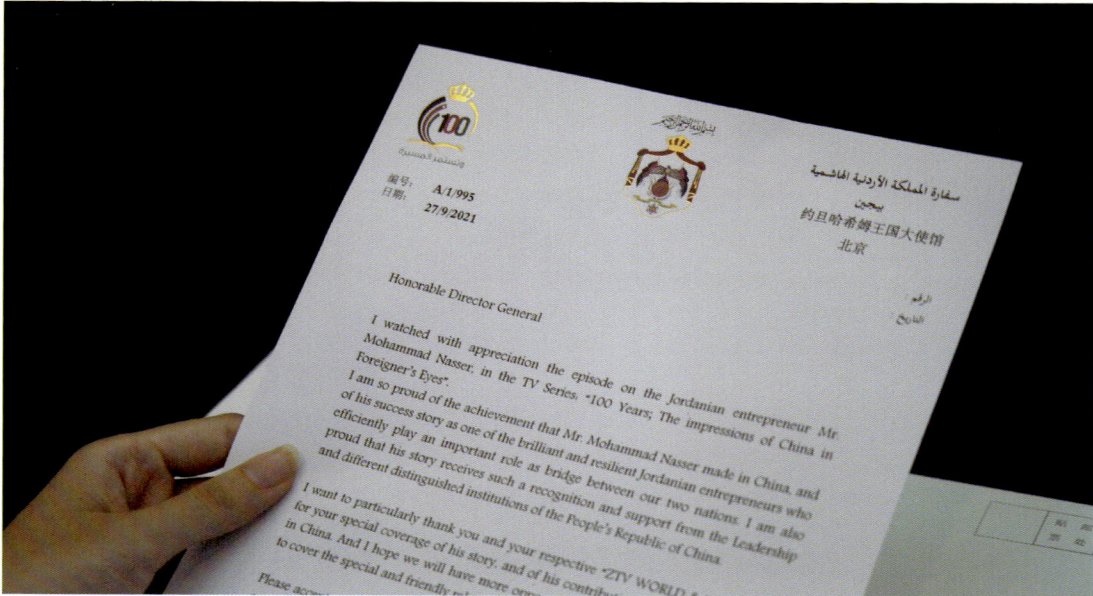

约旦驻华大使致信

A letter from Ambassador of the Hashemite Kingdom of Jordan to the People's Republic of China

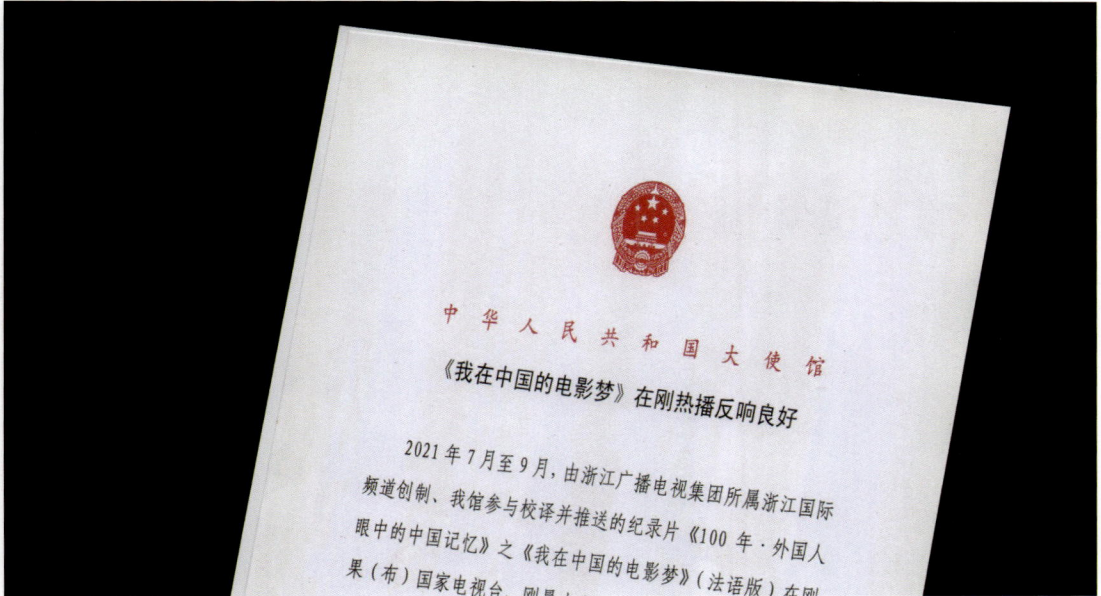

中国驻刚果共和国大使致信

A letter from Chinese Ambassador to the Republic of the Congo

江添文
Tim Clancy

　　我觉得这部影片很有教育意义，我对历史内容进行了相关的研究，懂得了很多，了解了在历史上发生了什么。我挺喜欢这部片子的。

江添文

《红船的故事》讲述者

　　I myself found it very educational, as I had to research lots of content and understand lots of things about what happened in the history. So, I'm quite happy with it.

Tim Clancy

The Narrator of *The Story of The Red Boat*

汤姆
Thomas Chapman

我能够亲身经历这段历史并跟这段历史有关的人交谈，我觉得这是一件很棒的事。

汤姆
《真理的味道》讲述者

To be able to talk to the people who were involved in and personally related to these stories, I think it's a great thing.

Thomas Chapman
The Narrator of *The Taste of Truth*

弗洛吉
Flogy Dostov

这不仅仅是关于我的故事，也是横店故事，中国故事。横店取得了如此多的成就，我们要以它为榜样。

弗洛吉
《我在中国的电影梦》讲述者

It's not just about me. It's about Hengdian, and it's about China. Hengdian achieved so many things that we need to take it as our example.

Ngalouo Flogy Dostov
The Narrator of *My Movie Dream in Hengdian, China*

彭国珍
Peng Guozhen

这个系列是一个很好的例子来展示如何讲好浙江故事，讲好中国故事。

彭国珍

浙江工业大学外国语学院院长

This program presents a great example to demonstrate how to better tell stories of Zhejiang and of China.

Peng Guozhen

Dean of College of Foreign Languages of Zhejiang University of Technology

李敏
Li Min

　　我认为国际学生可以成为文化交流的大使，他们可以根据个人经历去讲述中国故事。

李敏
浙江大学国际合作与交流处处长

I think international students could be cultural ambassadors, and they can tell the stories of China from their personal experiences.

Li Min
Director of Office of Global Engagement of Zhejiang University

魏克然
Vikram Channa

（这个系列）让观众们，尤其是我，能获得一些新的知识关于浙江的历史和中国共产党的历史。

魏克然
探索传媒集团副总裁

Our audience, me in particular, were able to discover some new facts of how to connect Zhejiang Province with the history of the CPC.

Vikram Channa
Vice President of Discovery Channel

功必扬
Brian Gonzalez

这个系列对国与国之间未来的发展和相互了解都非常重要。

功必扬
在华外籍青年代表

It will be very important for the future development and the mutual understanding between the two countries.

Brian Gonzalez
The Representative of Young Foreigners in China

黄亚洲
Huang Yazhou

它的叙述是软性的一种叙述，而不是一种硬性的宣传，我觉得这是这个影片很可贵的地方。

黄亚洲
著名作家、编剧

The narration is put in a soft approach rather than a blunt one, which is very valuable for this program.

Huang Yazhou
Famous Chinese Writer and Scriptwriter

杨明伟
Yang Mingwei

　　我觉得它的表达方式、内容选择上，它讲故事的形式上，符合总书记最近在中央政治局学习会上特别强调的，"要讲述一个可信的、可爱的、可敬的中国"这么一个要求。

杨明伟
中共中央党史和文献研究院对外合作交流局局长

I think the content and the way of expression and story-telling are in line with what General Secretary Xi Jinping emphasized recently at a group study session of the Political Bureau of the CPC Central Committee. He encouraged us to tell the story of a credible, loveable and respectable China.

Yang Mingwei
Director General of the International Communication and Exchanges Bureau of the Institute of Party History and Literature of the CPC Central Committee

胡萨姆·侯赛尼
Hussam Al Husseini

我们将进一步为加强两国之间的良好关系做出贡献。

胡萨姆·侯赛尼
约旦哈希姆王国驻华大使

We'll contribute even further to strengthening this excellent relationship between our two countries.

Hussam Al Husseini
Ambassador of the Hashemite Kingdom of Jordan to the People's Republic of China

《100 年·外国人眼中的中国浙江记忆》系列节目进高校
100 Years: The Impressions of Zhejiang, China in Foreigners' Eyes entered universities

驻外大使邀请当地主流媒体观看节目。

Chinese ambassadors to foreign countries have invited local mainstream media agencies to watch the program.

中国驻刚果民主共和国大使朱京邀请主流媒体观看《100年·外国人眼中的中国浙江记忆》
Chinese Ambassador to the Democratic Republic of the Congo invited mainstream media to watch
100 Years: The Impressions of Zhejiang, China in Foreigners' Eyes

　　节目已入选国家广电总局 2021 年"丝绸之路视听工程"项目库，并获得中美电影电视节"最佳电视纪录片"奖。

　　The program has been listed into the Audio Visual Projects of the Silk Road of the Chinese National Radio and Television Administration in 2021 and has won the "BEST TV DOCUMENTARY" of the 2021 Chinese American TV Festival.

入选国家广电总局
2021年"丝绸之路视听工程"项目库
The program has been listed into the Audio Visual Projects of the Silk Road
of the Chinese National Radio and Television Administration in 2021

2021 | Chinese American
TV Festival
Golden Angel Awards

BEST TV DOCUMENTARY

100 YEARS·THE IMPRESSIONS OF CHINA IN FOREIGNERS' EYES

中美電影節
Chinese American Film Festival

Chinese American TV Festival
中美電視節

James Su
Chairman

2021 中美电影电视节"最佳电视纪录片"奖获奖证书

Certificate of award for the "BEST TV DOCUMENTARY" of the 2021 Chinese American TV Festival.

节目已制作成多语种版本，已在刚果共和国国家电视台连续播出，并将在其他国家电视台播出。未来，它将作为文化交流的礼物，在浙江国际频道合作的海外播出窗口播出。

The program has been produced into multilingual versions and has been broadcasted on the national television of the Republic of Congo. It will also be broadcasted on other national televisions. In the future, it will serve as a gift for cultural exchange to ZTV WORLD's overseas broadcasting partners.

浙江国际频道始终致力于联通中外，沟通世界，讲好中国故事，传播中国声音。

ZTV WORLD has been working hard in connecting China with the rest of the world, sharing the stories of China and spreading the voice of China.

Camila Bianca Morello
Argentina (阿根廷)

Spanish
西班牙语

French
法语

Arabic language
阿拉伯语

Ilham Mounssif
Italy (意大利)

Italian
意大利语

多语种版本
Multilingual versions

主　创

黄　未　薛　晋　高　枫　郭　玥　楼冰莼

朱乐陶　刘　臻　张艺卓　张　磊　邹思嘉

图书在版编目（CIP）数据

100年·外国人眼中的中国浙江记忆 / 黄未，薛晋主编. -- 杭州：浙江大学出版社，2022.8
ISBN 978-7-308-22655-4

Ⅰ．①1… Ⅱ．①黄… ②薛… Ⅲ．①浙江－地方史－近现代 Ⅳ．①K295.5

中国版本图书馆CIP数据核字(2022)第087214号

100年·外国人眼中的中国浙江记忆

黄 未 薛 晋 主编

责任编辑	包灵灵
责任校对	田 慧 仝 林
封面设计	云水文化
出版发行	浙江大学出版社
	（杭州市天目山路148号　邮政编码　310007）
	（网址：http://www.zjupress.com）
排　　版	云水文化
印　　刷	杭州高腾印务有限公司
开　　本	710mm×1000mm　1/16
印　　张	15
字　　数	200千
版 印 次	2022年8月第1版　2022年8月第1次印刷
书　　号	ISBN 978-7-308-22655-4
定　　价	68.00元